Pictures from the Life of Nelson

CAPTAIN NELSON, 1781. AGE, 22.

From the Painting by J. F. Rigaud   By kind permission of Earl Nelson.

Pictures from the Life of Nelson

W. Clark Russell

NAVAL INSTITUTE PRESS
Annapolis, Maryland

Naval Institute Press
291 Wood Road
Annapolis, MD 21402

First Naval Institute Press edition 2005

Foreword © R. D. Madison, 2005
All rights reserved. No part of this book may be reproduced or
utilized in any form or by any means, electronic or mechanical,
including photocopying and recording, or by any information
storage and retrieval system, without permission in writing from
the publisher.

First edition 1897 by Dodd, Mead & Company

Library of Congress Cataloging-in-Publication Data
Russell, William Clark, 1844–1911.
     Pictures from the life of Nelson / by W. Clark Russell.
       p. cm.
     Originally published: New York : Dodd, Meade and Co.,
Publishers, 1879. With new foreword.
     ISBN 1-59114-746-8 (acid-free paper)
1. Nelson, Horatio Nelson, Viscount, 1758–1805. 2. Admirals—
Great Britain—Biography. I. Title.

DA87.1.N4R9 2005
940.2'7'092—dc22

2004058799

Printed in the United States of America on acid-free paper
12 11 10 09 08 07 06 05   9 8 7 6 5 4 3 2 ∞
First printing

CONTENTS

FOREWORD

In 1810 Robert Southey (1774–1843) wrote that "The best eulogium of Nelson is the history of his actions; the best history that which shall relate them most perspicuously." Today we would say "most clearly," and that, I think, is the difference between Southey's standard biography—read by every schoolboy in the nineteenth century—and the biography that began with the era of the American naval historian and biographer Alfred Thayer Mahan (1840–1914). Language and the focus of biography have changed radically since Southey wrote (making even his book hard to follow sometimes), but he is still right about one thing: the best way to talk about Nelson is simply to tell what he did.

And that's the second problem: readers who pick up a biography of Nelson will get more than they expect. Nelson's was a life brimming over with incident. He had been in more

than a hundred skirmishes with the French
even before his first great victory at the Nile.
He had already lost an eye and an arm. Biographers from Clarke and McArthur in 1809 to
William Clark Russell in 1890 wanted to
include it all.

Clark Russell (the double name sounds
awkward to us, but his contemporaries always
referred to him this way) was born in 1844 in
New York, but he was educated in Britain and
Europe. He went to sea at age thirteen and
became a thorough British tar. The story goes
that returning from sea at age twenty-three in
1867, he brought with him a manuscript of a
sea story—a genre made famous by Frederick
Marryat (1792–1848) and James Fenimore
Cooper (1789–1851). The London publisher
Sampson Low, Son & Marston took a chance
on the book, and Clark Russell began a second
career as a highly successful man of letters.
Another version of the story is that he gave up
the sea as early as age twenty-one. In either
case, he was impressively young to be pub-
lishing a novel. His few years at sea had
already taken their toll on his health, as life at
sea did to all seamen in the age of sail. A
forty-year-old sailor was indeed a shellback.

Clark Russell's breakthrough novel was *The Wreck of the Grosvenor* (1878), a storm-wracked work that proves that Christian piety and a good adventure story can exist side by side. Just three years later Clark Russell was seriously ill, but he continued to write profusely. His fame led him to a nearly decade-long correspondence with an aging Herman Melville (1819–91), whose early works had inspired him. Despite Melville's deep skepticism, the two men admired each other's work. Clark Russell recognized his friend's "wide and perhaps bitter experience," while Melville referred to Clark Russell's novels as "something yet better" than his own. In 1888 Melville dedicated *John Marr and Other Sailors,* a collection of poetry, to Clark Russell, and in 1890 Clark Russell in turn dedicated his next novel, *An Ocean Tragedy,* to Melville. Melville's last novel, *Billy Budd,* is a synthesis of the sea worlds of both authors. No wonder: Melville was reading Clark Russell's first Nelson biography in those last few creative months before his own death in 1891.

When asked to prepare a volume on Nelson for the Heroes of the Nations series edited by Evelyn Abbott (1843–1901), a Greek scholar at Oxford and brother of the mathematician and novelist Edwin Abbott (1838–1926), Clark Russell complied readily but recognized that he could never escape being under the shadow of Southey's still popular *Life of Nelson.* But because Clark Russell had written the greatest sea novel of his day, as well as many other works of maritime fiction and nonfiction, he was the logical person to write the biography of Britain's greatest naval hero—a biography to stand alongside volumes on heroic figures as diverse as Alexander the Great and Lincoln, Lorenzo de Medici and the Cid.

Clark Russell's 1890 Nelson biography, *Horatio Nelson and the Naval Supremacy of England,* is good and thorough and readable, but only in the chapters on the great battles do we see the greatest English sea writer between Marryat and Joseph Conrad (1857–1924) peeking through the cargo of detail. Naval ordnance expert William H. Jaques (1848–1916)—a writer for, among others, the U.S. Naval Institute *Proceedings* journal—contributed technical appendixes that neither fit Clark Russell's narrative nor clarified Nelson's achievement. If there were a Plimsoll line for books, this one wouldn't have been allowed to leave port. And Clark Russell, from kelson to truck, knew it.

Rarely in this life do writers have the opportunity to rectify their published mistakes, but Clark Russell did get the chance to improve upon his 1890 book. Six years after writing his first Nelson biography, as the Nelson centennial began, newspaper editor Clement K. Shorter (1857–1926) invited Clark Russell to write a more popular series of Nelson sketches for the *English Illustrated Magazine*. By now, Clark Russell had become familiar with Mahan's great work examining Nelson as a tactician, *The Life of Nelson: The Embodiment of the Sea Power of Great Britain* (1897). With Mahan's probing analysis before the public, and having already published his own "comprehensive" biography, Clark Russell was free to do what he could do best: simply tell the best stories.

Periodical publication helped him: every single chapter had to be a coherent whole; every word had to be understood by the English workingman. Falling back on his exceptional technique as a novelist, Clark Russell brought to life Nelson's dispatches and the rest of the documentary material that had been presented so formally in previous biographies, including his own of 1890. Without editorializing, Clark Russell's narrative voice comes through like that of an old mariner in love with the subject of heroism at sea as only a British seaman of the age of sail could express it.

Those serialized sketches were published in book form in 1897, under the title *Pictures from the Life of Nelson*. It was modest in both size and illustration compared to the much more comprehensive 1890 biography. It could just fit in the pocket of a pea jacket or be tucked away in a seabag. In the preface to this collected edition, Clark Russell acknowledged the examples of maritime realism that he so much appreciated—Cooper's *Ned Myers* (1843), written from the accounts of a broken-down shipmate of his boyhood days; Melville's *Redburn* (1849), the stylized autobiography of that author's first voyage; and *Two Years before the Mast* (1840), the narrative by Richard Henry Dana Jr. (1815–82) that moved sea literature from the cabin to the forecastle. Clark Russell wanted to portray Nelson as a common sailor—not that there was anything common about Nelson, but Clark Russell felt the exalted Nelson needed to be placed among the common sailors who were most intimately associated with his success. In a literary way, Clark Russell knew he had succeeded in taking the life of Nelson out of the parlors and into the shops and pubs.

After years of invalidism, Clark Russell died in 1911. He had lived to see his own reputation begin to fade as twentieth-century modernism, in the guise of Conrad's magnificent psychological examinations of the sea, began to drive out the sentimental piety of the romantic revival to which Clark Russell belonged. And yet, his achievement was solid, and his *Pictures from the Life of Nelson* is a minor classic. "Many lives of Nelson have been written," Southey had noted in 1810; "one is yet wanting, clear and concise enough to become a manual for the young sailor, which he may carry about with him, till he has treasured up the example in his memory and in his heart." Southey wrote that book for his generation, and with the timelessness of a novelist, Clark Russell—the Patrick O'Brian of his age—wrote his book for future generations.

R. D. MADISON

PREFACE

THESE short and slight excursions of my pen will be accepted as a little volume of water colours by a hand which is not an "expert's" nor naval in the military sense of the word; and if they are ill done there are plenty of critics to tell me so.

I was commissioned by Mr. Clement K. Shorter, the able editor of the "Illustrated London News," to write these articles, and I beg to thank him and the proprietors of the "English Illustrated Magazine" for their kindness in permitting me to reprint them. I have added as a supplement an article on the condition of our merchant seamen, which is most certainly not irrelevant whatever else it may be. In former times the navy and the merchant service were interdependent. We looked to the red flag for reinforcements, and merchant Jack helped us to win our greatest victories. Now, everything, as I have pointed out, is changed. The merchant ship on which we used to rely for seamen is filled with foreigners

who are of no earthly use to us as a fighting element. The shipowners act traitorously
towards their country in their quiet but insistent
elimination of the English merchant sailor from
British ships; but whatever is cheap is good
enough at sea as things stand, and no doubt in
a very short time there will not be in existence
such a thing as an English merchant sailor.
But this and more you will find set forth at
the end.

Everything fresh, true, and good about the
sea usually comes from America. In this
country we have had one sea-writer. He is
Marryat. At all events, we point to no other.
People who cannot discriminate or distinguish,
talk of Smollett as a naval novelist. He was
at sea for a very short time, and cruised amongst
the gallipots of the surgeon in the cockpit,
whose scenes he has painted with the brush of
a Hogarth. But he was no more a sailor than
the doctor who feels your pulse and looks at
your tongue. He never went aloft, knew nothing of navigation, probably could not have told
you swiftly and correctly the names of the sails
and rigging of a ship. But what he did, was
well done, and I wish there was more of it.

It is from America that the real sea-message
usually comes. We find it in Fenimore

Cooper's "Ned Myers," in Herman Melville's "Redburn," in the incomparable Dana's "Two Years before the Mast," and now in Captain Mahan's very instructive, abundant, and interesting "Life of Lord Nelson." Mahan has sought to do for his brilliant hero exactly what Dana has achieved for his humble merchant sailor of the "Pilgrim." In both cases the interpretation is very fine, but it must be remembered that Dana had not a glorious career to write about, had not a fascinating, voluptuous heroine to introduce. His genius is great and ever admirable, because he was the *first* to open the fore-scuttle and point with eloquent forefinger down into the merchant seaman's obscure, darksome, wet, miserable home. It was a revelation! It was the life of thousands of toilers of whose very existence people ashore knew nothing. Many great men in this country were eager and ardent in their recognition of it, — Charles Dickens, Bulwer Lytton, Carlyle, amongst others. All these men wrote flattering letters to Dana, who has rendered humanity so great a service that nothing short of a public statue erected to his famous memory in the city of Boston could sufficiently express the gratitude that is due, and by all thoughtful seafarers, felt.

Mahan's " Nelson" touches the other pole. It reads like a novel, and Cooper could not have made it more interesting. It, too, is a revelation in its way, and it is not only a very great monument to the author's industry, it is packed full of everything that has been said about Nelson at all trustworthy, and it is also one of the finest literary compliments the United States have ever paid this country.

The life of Nelson consists of anecdotes, incidents, battles, and so forth. All the stories have been told over and over again. It would be unwise to say anything that is new, because it would not be true. It is hard, therefore, in the face of generations of biographers to find freshness of colour for these Pictures of Nelson. Stanier Clarke, Southey, and other biographers of Nelson, have told the stories of his life, have related the incidents, even the most dramatic incidents, of his career, with little ambition of " colourishment," as Sir Thomas Browne would say. Nelson's latest biographers attempt no more. The same stories and the same death-bed scene are to be found in all the books. How can we give freshness to such a worn canvas ? Of all the lives before the public the one that is most sure of lasting, in my opinion, is Southey's. We read it when we were children, our children read it; it is a national book, and we love it. The best edition I know is Mr. David Hannay's, and I commend it and its valuable appendices with sincere pleasure, because Mr. David Hannay is the able son of the author of " Singleton Fontenoy," a gallant, true, beautiful, scholarly marine story, and a handsome and a sufficient effort to neutralise the degrading caricatures of our Scotch friend, Tobias the profane.

One page of graphic description is worth whole shelves of insipid narrative. This was my opinion when, in my " Life of Nelson " published by Messrs. Putnam's of New York, I quoted in full, as I quote in these pages, Lieutenant Parsons' picture of Nelson on board his ship when in chase of the " Généreux," one of the two line-of-battle ships which had escaped from the Nile. Captain Mahan has also, I observe, quoted in full this description, without, however, referring to his authority. One wants to know how they fought in Nelson's time. We can think of nothing but the ironclad and the torpedo in this age. The historian whose periods never sent a boy to sea, but who is scrupulously accurate in his dates (mostly, I mean), who is very strong and even fierce in his opinions on naval matters, though his books

sell chiefly in " remainders," will tell you that
the action began at noon, but by the log of the
" Hesperus " it began at three seconds past
noon, by the log of the " Pinafore " at twenty
seconds past noon, and then the " Dido "
delivered a broadside, and the Frenchman or
the Yankee fired a broadside in return. You
hear nothing, you see nothing, you feel nothing.
On the printed page before you are a number
of black marks with black lines attached
to them signifying the positions of ships at
various times in the engagement, and in this
age of ironclads and thirty-knot torpedo-
catchers these black marks suggest nothing so
much as black beetles, whose tactics in escaping
the printed page would be to the full as lumi-
nous, instructive, and certainly as humorous, as
the lesson of the historian's diagrams.

Here is a description of a fight which I commend to the attention of the " experts," who
will not fail to admire this admirable picture.
In 1801 despatches were received at the Admiralty by the Norfolk Packet. One letter
ran thus : —

SIR, — I have the honour to acquaint you, that on
January 1st, 1801, I worked his Majesty's ship the
" Desdemona " out of Chesapeake Bay in company with
the republican French frigate " Le Fripon " ; and having

gained a sufficient offing to come to battle, we commenced close action; when the superior metal of the enemy caused the " Desdemona " to make so much water that the carpenter informed me the Ship was going down. Upon hearing this I called my boarders, and carried the enemy in the smoke. Every officer, seaman and marine, did their duty. I regret the loss of. . . .

> I am &c.,
>
> BRYAN BRILLIANT.

The story runs thus : —

" The French frigate had now weighed, and stood out of the bay, with her jack, ensign, and pennant flying; nor did an interval of a minute elapse before the anchor of the ' Desdemona ' was hove up to the bow, and sail made on the ship.

" No sooner had both ships gained an offing, than the French frigate hauled up her foresail, took in her topgallant sails, and hove to for the ' Desdemona,' whose inferiority of sailing was manifest, and who was crowding every inch of canvas to come within gunshot of her opponent. Upon which Captain Brilliant took in his royals, and his ship's company manning the shrouds, gave three hearty cheers. . . .

" The men, fore and aft, were now at their quarters, and Captain Brilliant, looking over the break of the quarter-deck, vociferated to them through his speaking-trumpet,

"' Stand by, my boys!'

"' All ready!' was the reply.

"Upon which our hero ran up alongside the French frigate; and calling to his people 'Fire away!' they discharged their broadside, which was returned by the enemy before the sound was out of the 'Desdemona's' guns.

"The action thus begun was continued on board the 'Desdemona' with that cool intrepidity which is the distinguishing characteristic of British seamen; and Captain Brilliant proved that he was both a sailor and an officer, for he both worked and fought his own ship.

"And on the quarter-deck of glory were to be seen, the master anticipating the orders of the captain; the marine officer firing his division over the quarter, and Lieutenant Hurricane calling to the men at the quarter-deck guns and carronades, 'Keep yourselves cool, my lads! Mind the heave of the sea! Now strike it into her!'

"The two ships had now got close to each other, exchanging their compliments yard-arm and yard-arm; a practice introduced by Benbow, and revived by Anson. At this period, the hammocks in the quarter-deck nettings of the

' Desdemona ' caught fire from a wad of the enemy ; upon which a young midshipman jumped from his gun, and lugging out his knife, cut them away overboard.

" ' Bravo ! ' exclaimed Captain Brilliant — but before he could utter more, an eighteen-pound shot tore up the bulwark and made the splinters fly in every direction, laying flat on the deck, some on their backs and some on their faces, the following officers and men : —

Robert Soundings, Master.

Francis Easy, The Marine Officer.

Thomas Wilson, Quartermaster.

John Pearce, Captain of the after-guard.

Hugh Vincent, Ordinary Seaman; and

Mars Mattocks, A Marine.

" ' Jump here ! bear a hand ! ' vociferated Lieutenant Hurricane, ' and carry Mr. Soundings into the cockpit. A blasted shot that ! Messmate, are you much wounded ? '

" ' I fear,' faltered the master, ' my grog is stopped.'

" ' And how are you, my dear Easy ? ' said Hurricane.

" ' I feel,' replied the marine officer, ' I shall have to capitulate ! Death has already put his storming-ladder to my soul ! I die ! I die ! My God ! My God ! '

" ' Are you much hurt, Pearce?' inquired Hurricane.

" ' Yes, sir,' replied the captain of the after-guard, ' that shot cut away my life-lines! My soul is unreeving! O Peggy! Peggy! My wife! my dear wife!'

" About this period the colours of the enemy disappeared.

" ' She has struck!' cried an Irish landsman in the waist.

" ' Struck!' retorted Captain Brilliant. ' By heaven! You may strike first yet. Does she slacken fire? Is it the guns or the colours you judge by?'

" The captain had scarce finished speaking when a new pair of colours were hoisted by the enemy. Her ensign had been shot away.

" A sailor from each of the quarter-deck guns had now left his station, to carry the wounded down into the cockpit; and a couple of stout lads had got hold of the master, whom they were lugging to the hatchway.

" ' Avast there!' cried Captain Brilliant, ' with the master. He has struck. The soul of as good a seaman as ever took hold of the helm of a vessel is gone aloft to Heaven!'

" ' Jump to the marine officer,' cried Lieutenant Hurricane.

"'By —— !' said Captain Brilliant, 'it is of no use. The marine officer has resigned his commission. Look to Pearce, the captain of the after-guard. How is it with him?'

"'He is gone, sir,' replied Lieutenant Hurricane, 'upon the same tack as the marine officer. He has answered the muster of death.'

"At this juncture a crash was heard in the main deck, which was followed by doleful groans.

"'Jump,' said the captain, 'into the waist! the Frenchman's shot is playing at hell and turn-up-Jack there!'

"The midshipman soon returned.

"'A shot, sir, has dismounted one of the midship guns, killed the third lieutenant, and wounded almost every man at the gun.'

"'What!' cried Lieutenant Hurricane, 'has death dropped the peak of my messmate, poor Balcony?'

"'Huzza! my sons!' cried Captain Brilliant to the people at the main-deck guns. 'Beauty! that's the fire!'

"The exhortations of Captain Brilliant were interrupted by the carpenter. He came upon deck to acquaint the captain that the enemy's shot had taken such effect that there were several feet of water in the well; and that even if recourse were had to the pumps, it would be impracticable to keep the ship half an hour above water.

" ' Be it so, Mr. Chips,' said the captain. ' But hark you! Say not a word about the matter. I will soon have a clear well.'

" The two frigates were now so close alongside of one another that their yard-arms were mutually locked by their rigging.

" ' Hurricane,' cried Captain Brilliant, ' I will board the Frenchman in the smoke. Hark you! call the boarders. I will put myself at their head. In the mean time, be ready yourself to follow me with a fresh gang of volunteers.'

" The boarders now assembled to the amount of seventy, — men equal to any heroic enterprise, men who would have gone through flames, had their duty imposed on them the task. They were armed with cutlasses and pistols.

" ' Are you ready, my sons?' cried Captain Brilliant.

" ' All ready, sir,' was the reply.

" ' Then follow me!' cried the hero.

" Captain Brilliant now boarded the enemy's ship, followed by his men, who were all contending for the honour of fighting by his side.

" The French officers and sailors collected to oppose the assailants. But such was the discipline, such the intrepidity of the British tars,

that resistance was of no avail. Brilliant, with
his troop of boarders, made his way through
a host of enemies. The first lieutenant followed
in succession with volunteers from the ship's
company ; and the ' Desdemona,' like the fabled
horse of Troy, poured out heroes from her
womb !

"The Frenchmen called for quarter. But
before they had made the supplication a midshipman had got aft and hauled down their
colours."

This is a striking old-fashioned sea-piece worthy of being hung alongside Lieutenant Parsons' picture, which I have quoted in these
pages. The descriptions show us how they
fought in the days of Nelson. It is a forsaken
art because it is no longer necessary. The Bril-
liants of to-day will not fight their ships as they
did when admirals and captains were dependent
on the wind. It is sad to reflect that Nelson's
tactics, which gave us our marine supremacy,
should be of no use to us. They sank out of
sight, paralysed by the stroke of the propeller.
When steam came in the tactics of tacks and
sheets went out. Would an admiral think of
cutting the line when he knows that what used to
be called the leewardmost ships could steam up

Preface

to the rescue or help of their friends at the rate
of sixteen or twenty knots an hour? Every
wind is a fair wind for the steamer. But old
sea officers and naval schoolmasters cannot
submit to be told that the change is absolute.
They cling with pathetic affection to the obso-
lete methods; for them the wind continues to
howl in the shrouds. If they say it was a bad
day for England when the ironclad was introduced, and when the old wooden battle-ship was
sent to the knackers, most thoughtful people
will agree with them. The ironclad is not
likely to produce the splendid set of sailors who
were at sea in Nelson's day. How can you
make sailors out of ships in which there is no
work for a sailor to do? But one thing is universally believed: that if the tactics of Nelson
are as dead as his hallowed ashes, his glorious
memory survives to inspire the British seaman.

In ordinary sea-manœuvres also, steam has
wrought an astounding change. Let us take
the case of a ship in a gale of wind on a lee
shore. I will instance the steamer first. In
March, 1889, H. M. S. "Calliope," with several
warships of other nations, was anchored in Apia
Bay in the Island of Samoa. It came on to
blow a gale of wind; the gale grew into a hurricane of cyclonic power. The situation of the

ships was one of frightful danger. They lay embayed and crowded like sheep. Captain Kane, the commander of the "Calliope," formed his resolution ; he would steam out and secure an offing if he could. All the seamanship here required lay in the captain's resolution. The work was to be done by the engineers and the engines. Her struggle, as she was thrust out, scarcely making a mile an hour through the enormous head seas, has been graphically described. Captain Kane conned his ship with great judgment, and eventually gained the open sea with but little material loss worth mentioning. This is how it is done in the days of steam.

Let us see how it was done in the days of sail. On the evening of the 16th September, 1812, H. M. S. " Magnificent," a line-of-battle ship of seventy-four guns, anchored between Chasseron and the Isle of Rhé, in the neighbourhood of Basque Roads. Before the sails were furled, the weather looking threatening, a reef was taken in the courses, and the topsails were close reefed. The wind increased, and the topgallant yards were got down upon deck. They veered cable to a cable and a half, on the best bower anchor, by which the ship was riding in sixteen fathoms of water. Shortly before ten the anchor *broke* and the small bower was let go, which brought the ship up in ten fathoms. "The yards and topmasts were immediately struck. The night was dark, but the sea breaking on the reef made a light by which an awful view of the ship's dangerous position was obtained. The best bower was now unspliced, and the inner cable bent to the spare anchor. The slack of the best bower was then hove in to about two thirds of a cable, and the anchor, fouling a rock, helped to hold the ship. It was, therefore, 'bitted' and secured." A leadsman was in the port chains getting a cast of the lead every five minutes. A quartermaster stood at the starboard gangway attending the deep-sea lead, which was probably on the ground over the side to show if she drifted. Large rocks were now seen close under the ship. She was without chain cables, and it was known that her hemp cables would certainly chafe through in a few hours. A wild broken sea was running, so jerking the ship that the oars were occasionally thrown out of the barge on the booms.

"When every preparation had been made, — the officers and men in their respective stations, ready to act on the shortest notice, — the captain placed himself in the port gangway, to watch the heaving of the hand-lead. The gale, accompanied by rain, continued with unabated force, and the heavy sea breaking upon the reef astern, produced frightful flashes, which, in the darkness of the night, rolling over the rocks, might have been likened to moving masses of liquid fire."

The day had scarcely dawned when the quartermaster, attending the deep-sea lead, declared the ship to be driving. The spare anchor was instantly let go, which providentially brought her up again; nevertheless it was but too certain that the ship could not be held much longer by cables which had been chafing so many hours on sharp and rugged rocks. The wind was now at west; St. Marie Church, on Isle Rhé, bore east. The gale increased; but the favourable change in the wind was counterpoised by a strong lee current, and a heavy cross-sea on the off-shore bow. The sun had already reached the meridian, unaccompanied by any indication of a favourable change in the weather; and the captain feeling it impossible to sustain through another long night the intense anxiety of that of the preceding, thus addressed the French pilot: —

"Pilot, can you save the ship?" "By gare, no!" was the desponding reply of the foreigner. Orders were then given to sway up the lower

Preface

yards to three fourths of their *usual height*, — to secure the topmasts close down, leaving the topsail yards to work on the caps, — to pass the largest hawser through the starboard quarter-port, and to bend it to the cable on the spare anchor, for the purpose of acting as a spring in canting the ship to port, previously to cutting the cables; but, at the instant of bending the hawser, the cable *parted*, and it was ultimately bent to the small bower cable.

The courses and topsails were secured in three or four places, on their respective yards, with stops of spun-yarn, so as to be cut on the instant; the gaskets had been previously cast off: the head and main yards were braced up for the starboard tack, and the other yards kept square, dividing the men (who would otherwise have been required at the braces) between the fore-tack, and fore and fore-topsail sheets.

It will be seen, that in the event of the spring casting the ship, the head yards would require no alteration, and it would only be necessary to guard against setting their sails *too soon*. On the other hand, if the spring (which was every way probable) broke, the yards could not be better placed for producing the sternboard, which would in that case be necessary to clear the reef.

The spring was hove in to a tolerable strain. The master was directed to attend at the bitts, and see that the carpenters cut the cables the instant the word was given. All being ready, and the greater number of those on board being in the expectation of a watery grave, the cables were cut. The heavy sea on the port-bow acting against the spring, caused it to snap : it was immediately cut by the axe provided for that purpose, to prevent retarding the ship's sternway : the helm was put hard to starboard — the fore-topmast staysail hoisted — the fore-topsail let fall, and sheeted home — the foresail let fall — the tack boarded and the sheet roused aft. All the sail was flat aback and *set in less than half a minute*. The ship's head paid round quickly towards the reef. When the wind was abaft the beam, the mizzen-topsail was let fall, and sheeted home, and the helm shifted. When the wind came right aft, the main topsail was let fall, and sheeted home : the mainsail was next loosed, the tack boarded, the sheet roused aft, and the mizzen-topsail, cross-jack, and main topsail yards braced up for the starboard tack.

This manœuvre, from the cutting of the spring till the requisite sails were set, did not exceed *two minutes*. At the moment that the ship's head was in the direction of the rocks, and then only in five fathoms water, the vessel made a desperate plunge, and in hauling to the wind the send of the sea did not leave, by the soundings, more than a single foot of water under the keel.

The ship was shortly afterwards safely anchored in Basque Roads.

This is taken from a " Manual," dead as the gallant hand that planned it. It excellently describes a most masterful manœuvre. Old sailors will follow the evolutions with enjoyment ; but to young sailors bred in steam, much of the language must necessarily be blank as Chinese. They were giants as fighting men ; they were giants as sailor men, and those were the days of Nelson. As the manœuvres of H. M. S. " Magnificent" are to the manœuvres of H. M. S. " Calliope," so are the tactics of Nelson to the tactics which will be adopted in the next naval battle.

I am fully in agreement with those who lament the general ignorance of naval history throughout the country. There should be no literature more fascinating. Why is it not so ? Why do not schoolboys greedily devour studies and histories of old heroes and old wars and their causes and results ? The truth is, if naval history is unpopular and unread, it is because it does unfortunately fall into the hands of men who

are not artists and who are incapable of writing
so as to engage and delight. Mr. Laird Clowes'
" The Royal Navy " should prove a popular
work because he is importing colour, and life,
and light, and movement into its pages. Dry
bones are made to live again, and one follows
the narrative (by several hands) as a romance
of the sea. But what naval histories have we
which are not dull and disgusting? What
naval history is likely to attract the attention
of the young, who want the story told with
breadth, force, and knowledge, in language
coloured with the spirit of its subject? What
boy would or could sit down and read James?

The world expected much from Professor
Laughton when it was reported that he was
writing a " Life of Nelson." The " Life "
appeared, I read it, and I mourned. Professor
Laughton is not an artist; he has no sense of
proportion or of keeping; he loads his slender
page with an account of the Sucklings, then
seems to follow my suggestion in asking where
Nelson got his fighting spirit from; and he
agrees with me that the stories told about
Nelson's boyhood are scarcely worth recalling.
or crediting. It is a very accurate little book,
but uncommonly dry; the schoolmaster and
the critic are visible in every line; he is perpet-

Preface

ually breaking away from his subject to quarrel with or correct the opinions of others, which I submit is not biography but criticism. And yet I understand that this author is among others who lament that naval history is unread in this country.

I may add that these papers were written in the middle of 1896.

W. CLARK RUSSELL.

Bath, 1897.

Pictures from the Life of Nelson

Pictures from the Life of Nelson

CHAPTER I

EARLY BOYHOOD

WHAT genius of the brush will give us a
picture of little Nelson wandering in
Chatham Dockyard in search of the " Raisonnable," a big ship of sixty-four guns commanded by
Captain Suckling, and filled with pigtails and
petticoat trousers? One need but close one's
eyes to behold the vision in its completeness,
pale in the ghostly sunshine of a long vanished
day. The weather is bleak, the year is 1771.
The London coach is late. Presently it thunders up to the door of the hostelry, and there
alights a delicate little boy, attenuated and pale,
eyes brilliant with genius, and a countenance of
charming refinement shadowed by the sadness
of leave-taking.

A boy going to sea! How very different, to
be sure, his aspect, and the suggestions of it,
from those traditional ideas of boys going to sea

which we receive into our minds from the inimitable, licentious, and libellous Tobias! This boy should sport a grog-blossom for a nose, his hair should hang in a shower of carrot-parings; though but a weanling, his utterance should be as coarse as his teeth, and his profanity as vigorous as the coachman's. How he is dressed I am not able to tell you; his father is a poor country parson, and the lad's outfit is a slender one. You do not need to be told that he is a young gentleman; you see breeding in his hands and face, in the turns of his head, in the motions of his little form.

Now he has to find the " Raisonnable," a big King's ship, all of the olden time; and this little lad, who in all probability had never seen a real ship in his life, stares about him with the fascinated eyes of childhood as he walks. Did the love of the sea come to this boy through his mother, on whose side lay some gallant historic memory of ocean-struggle borne upon the page of naval record in the tale of Galfridus Walpole's action in the Mediterranean in 1711? Was the passion for the sea inherent, as it is in most English boys? In spite of his love of sailing paper boats in the market gutter at Downham, it may be credited that this boy's motive in going to sea was to relieve his father from the burden of maintaining him. Some who lived nearer to his time than we have so said. The Rev. Edmund Nelson was at Bath when little Horatio, in the pleasant rectory-house at Burnham Thorpe, sitting at table with his brother William, asked him — that is, William, who, through this same bright-eyed little chap, was raised to the peerage as an Earl long afterwards — to write to his father for permission to go to sea with Uncle Maurice Suckling. The reverend gentleman had consented; and what was Captain Suckling's answer? "What has poor Horace done, that he, above all the rest, should be sent to rough it out at sea? But let him come; and the first time we go into action a cannon-ball may knock off his head and provide for him at once."

Little Nelson did not seem able to find the "Raisonnable" very easily. He was bewildered by the shipping, by the complicated smells, by the tempestuous roaring voices of the Jacks, by a scene which is not now, as it certainly was not then, quite so delectable as the Bower that stood by Bendemeer's Stream. While he was looking at a hulk that was the home of hundreds of men, women, and children, though in her day her 'tween decks had thundered many fateful messages to the enemies of this country, a naval officer who had been watching him approached and asked him what he wanted. The youngster answered that he was in search of the "Raisonnable." "Captain Suckling?" says the naval officer. "Yes," answered Horatio. "He is my uncle, sir." "I know him very well. Yonder is the 'Raisonnable.' Her captain is not in Chatham, and may not be here for some days. Have you dined?" "No, sir," answered young Nelson. "You look cold and hungry. Come along home with me," said the kind-hearted officer, viewing with great interest not unmingled with pity the pale and delicate face of the lad. He marched him to his home, and presently he and Horatio, and perhaps kindly Mrs. Officer, and maybe — let us hope for the sake of posterity — several young Officers, were seated at table with a leg of mutton smoking in the midst of them and a good pudding to follow. I do not say that the embryo hero and his kind friend conversed exactly as I have written, but depend upon it something answering to this brief imaginary talk had being in that cold day and in that dockyard. After a good meal, which warmed the poor little fellow's heart, he went on board the "Raisonnable."

He had been rated by Captain Suckling as midshipman. Old Patronage was then flourishing in full vigour of limb and body. Is the giant dead? I believe with George Eliot that old Leisure is buried, but I fancy that even in these regenerated days of stern professors, stiff examinations, naval schools, and training-ships, a sort of tremble will now and again be seen to pass through old Patronage's form, and one eye will open and shut suddenly in a wink. By Patronage in those days hundreds obtained easy entrance into the Navy, and hundreds easy promotion. Young Nelson undoubtedly had interest at his back; Professor Laughton, in his brief "Life of Nelson," tells us that according to the "Instructions" Horatio should have been rated as the captain's servant. There was no dream of degradation in the term. It was just a *façon de parler*, — a well understood fiction; a young lord, the representative perhaps of a ducal house, might be entered as a servant. Be this as it will, Nelson undoubtedly started on his career as midshipman. The boy was twelve years old, having been born Sept. 29, 1758, and we are now dealing with the early month of the year 1771.

What sort of reception did he meet with when he gained the decks of the ship? Was his little lean frame much derided? Were coarse jokes hurled at him by riggers discoloured

with rum and by seamen with their back hair
lying between their shoulder-blades, just as it
had been tenderly combed and made ship-shape
by Soosie and Poll, who had left Wapping Old
Stairs to dwell in Chatham until the "Raisonnable" sailed? Some of Nelson's biographers tell
us that he wandered about the decks forlorn and
melancholy, pining for his home, and that his
young heart yearned for the old rectory, for his
father and brother, and for the simple interests
of his childish life. Who should doubt it?
There is just as much human nature in the
incipient hero as there is in the average boy
who will never cut a figure, and whose manli-
ness is not equal to the suppression of loud
blubbering when his clinging mother says,
"God bless you, my darling," and reluctantly,
with many parting looks, leaves him to the
loving care of the Reverend Doctor Cane.
Nelson could weep both as man and boy, and
he could also be seasick, and one loves him the
better for such weaknesses, for a perfect hero,
after the pattern of the Iron Duke, may appeal
to the admiration, but never to the affection, of
poor humanity.

It moves one to pity to figure a delicate little
boy reared to think with tender reverence and
love of the Supreme and of all that is right and

pure in life, on board a war-ship of that date. The calling of the Navy was, perhaps, never before nor since so rough. The pressgangs had been doing bloody business in London and the out-ports; and tenders were filled with merchantmen (and others who did not know what a ship was like), with their heads full of holes from the bludgeons of men who knew how to use both the cutlass and the pike. " I was disarmed," says Smollett, speaking in the person of Roderick Random, " taken prisoner, and carried on board a pressing tender, where, after being pinioned like a malefactor, I was thrust down into the hold among a parcel of miserable wretches, the sight of whom well-nigh distracted me. As the commanding officer had not humanity enough to order my wounds to be dressed, and I could not use my own hands, I desired one of my fellow captives who was unfettered to take a handkerchief out of my pocket and tie it round my head to stop the bleeding. He pulled out my handkerchief, 'tis true, but, instead of applying it to the use for which I designed it, went to the grating of the hatchway, and with astonishing composure sold it before my face to a bum-boat woman then on board, for a quart of gin with which he treated my companions, regardless of my circumstances and entreaties." The brutalising effect of the pressgang, even in this century when something of moderation was exercised, and when even something of humanity governed the thrust of the cutlass or the blow of the stick, may be read at large in the works of Marryat and Michael Scott. Strange that we should be obliged to turn to the pages of the novelists for the real historic record! But most historians of our Navy so much concern themselves with dates and the contradiction of other people's statements that they quite forget to be interesting.

The sailor, then, of Nelson's day was a very rough man indeed, with little love for his calling, but always fighting splendidly, for prize money first, and next for the preservation of his ship and the annihilation of the enemy. His ship was as rough as he was. Smollett draws a Hogarthian picture of the cockpit, where the midshipmen's quarters were situated: " We descended by divers ladders to a space as dark as a dungeon, which I understood was immersed several feet under water, being immediately above the hold. I had no sooner approached this dismal gulf than my nose was saluted with an intolerable stench of putrefied cheese and rancid butter that issued from an apartment at the foot of the ladder, resembling a chandler's shop, where, by the faint glimmering of a candle, I could perceive a man with a pale meagre countenance, sitting behind a kind of desk, having spectacles on his nose and a pen in his hand. This (I learned of Mr. Thomson) was the ship's steward, who sat there to distribute provisions to the several messes, and to mark what each received. He therefore presented my name to him and desired I might be entered in his mess; then taking a light in his hand, conducted me to the place of his residence, which was a square of about six feet, surrounded with the medicine-chest, that of the first mate, his own, and a board by way of table fastened to the after powder-room; it was also enclosed with canvas nailed round to the beams of the ship, to screen us from the cold, as well as from the view of the midshipmen and quartermasters who lodged within the cable tiers on each side of us." A glimpse of the midshipman and his quarters, a little earlier perhaps than Nelson's time, may be got by reading some forgotten verses written by William Falconer, the poet of the "Shipwreck." He thus speaks of the cockpit: —

> Deep in that fabric where Britannia boasts
> O'er seas to waft her thunder and her hosts
> A cavern lies! unknown to cheering day,
> Where one small taper lends a feeble ray.

After some lines not relevant to my purpose, Falconer gives us this description of a midshipman of a date but little anterior to Nelson's, dressing himself for dinner : —

> In neighbouring mansions, lo! what clouds arise! —
> It half conceals its owner from our eyes;
> One penny light with feeble lustre shines,
> To prove the Mid in high Olympus dines.
> Let us approach — the preparation view —
> A cockpit-beau is surely something new.
> To him Japan her varnish'd joys denies,
> Nor bloom for him the sweets of Eastern skies ;
> His rugged limbs no lofty mirror shows,
> Nor tender couch invites him to repose.
> A pigmy glass upon his toilet stands,
> Crack'd o'er and o'er by awkward, clumsy hands ;
> Chesterfield's page polite, the "Seaman's Guide,"
> An half-eat biscuit, Congreve's "Mourning Bride,"
> Bestrew'd with powder, in confusion lie,
> And form a chaos to the intruding eye.
> At length this meteor of an hour is dress'd,
> And rises an Adonis from his chest.
> Cautious he treads lest some unlucky slip
> Defiles his clothes with burgou or with flip ;
> These rocks escaped, arrives in statu quo,
> Bows ; dines, and bows ; then sinks again below.

By the dimly revealing gleam of this poetic rush-light we obtain a sort of insight into the hidden life of the man-of-war of old days, and can easily guess at the scene of confusion, smells, high jinks, the hectoring, craven bully of the mess into which little Nelson, fresh from the peaceful atmosphere of a country rectory, was to be introduced. It is to be lamented that we do not know who, if any, took him by the hand — how, in short, the little fellow " managed " until the arrival of the captain of the vessel. One would hope to find some reference to Nelson at this critical moment in a letter, an entry, a record of memory set down afterwards out of love for the glory the little man in later years achieved.

Certainly few things are more interesting in naval biography than the story of the introduction of the subjects of the lives into the sea career. Three instances occur to me. When John Jervis, afterwards the famous Earl of St. Vincent, the Admiral of St. Valentine's Day, first went on board his ship, his reception was such that his biographer, Captain Brenton, found himself incapable of describing it. "I have too much respect," he says, "for my readers to describe the scene which his Lordship presented to me, in a very few words, but in his clear and emphatic manner. Suffice it to say that in point of gross immorality and vice it equalled or outdid anything described by Smollett in his 'Roderick Random.'" It is difficult to understand what Brenton means by "gross immorality and vice." There is surely nothing immoral or vicious in the cockpit scenes depicted by Smollett. Of coarseness there is plenty, and also a great plenty of swearing. Captain Brenton was a religious man of a mild and charitable cast of nature, and it is possible that he found something more significant in the Earl's statement than a rougher sailor would have noticed. Perhaps there was something in young Jervis's dress that tickled the rude humour of his messmates. He wore a coat that had been made for him to grow up to. The skirts fell to his heels, and the sleeves were turned up half the length of the arm. Strap a dirk to this shape and fix something laced on its head, and caricature might not be able to make the figure more ridiculous. That many such grotesquely clad naval officers were afloat in those days and long subsequently we are well assured. A portrait drawn from the life may be found in "Old Bloody Politeful," the first lieutenant of a corvette, in "The Cruise of the Midge." Another instance of the introduction into the sea life is Collingwood's. The archness of the humour of that valorous North from whose loins Collingwood sprang and whose dark rolling Tyne and Wear have yielded us the grandest race of seamen the world has ever seen or shall see, may be found in the descriptions given in Collingwood's correspondence. Young Cuthbert went on board his ship and sat down upon a gun and began to cry bitterly over his separation from home. His misery was exquisite; he yearned for compassion and sympathy. Presently the first lieutenant accosted him with a note of kindness in his voice. This so affected the boy that he eagerly begged the officer to accompany him to his sea-chest, out of which he took a plum-cake and offered a large piece to the lieutenant.

Another instance is that of Lord Dundonald, then Lord Cochrane. His introduction was truly extraordinary. He found the first lieutenant dressed in the garb of a seaman, with his hair tied down his back, a marline-spike in one hand and a lump of grease in the other. This strange figure was busily occupied in setting up the main rigging. His name was Jack Larmour, and he had been promoted from the forecastle to the quarter-deck, to which part of the ship he had brought all the airs and graces of the land of the slush lamp and the evil-smelling mess-kid. Dundonald stood over six feet high; the lieutenant had heard that he was to have entered the army, and he surveyed the tall lean figure

with contempt. "Get your traps below!"
then roared Larmour. "This Lord Cochrane's
chest? Does Lord Cochrane think he's going
to bring a cabin aboard? The service is going
to the devil!" He then sent for the key of
the young nobleman's chest, and presently a
noise of sawing was to be heard. In fact, the
lieutenant ordered the chest to be sawn into
halves, "accompanying the operation," says
Lord Dundonald, "by sundry uncomplimentary
observations on midshipmen in general and on
myself in particular."

This sort of usage was not calculated to reconcile a boy to his friends' choice of a sea life.
The tender age and physical delicacy of little
Nelson doubtless pleaded for him and rescued
him from the rough and coarse people among
whom he had cast his lot. If he had nothing
to do until Captain Suckling arrived, there was
always the ship to look at. What a man-of-
war's hull resembled in those days may be easily
imagined by viewing the old "Victory" as she
lies at her moorings off Portsmouth. The white
bands were not then in use; they were yellow,
and often the ships were wholly black. It was
Nelson who introduced the band broken by the
gun-ports. The "Victory," as we know her, lacks
certain curly head-ornamentations such as are

familiar to us in paintings of old ships. I suspect that the old "Raisonnable" was a perfect bed
of head-boards, whence her long bowsprit and
jibboom forked upward in a steeve that made
them resemble a fourth mast very severely stayed
forward. She would have great round tops,
that is to say, platforms fitted a little below the
lower mast-head. In these tops the sailors
could have given a ball. The cat-harpings
complicated the gear aloft to the eye; everything was thick and massive. The shrouds
were like hawsers, and they descended into
channels filled with immense dead-eyes. But
the wonderful precision and neatness of the
British man-of-war would everywhere be visible.

One thinks of little Nelson as moving about
gazing at the guns, watching the riggers, staring
at the apparatus by which the heavy anchors
were hove up to the yawning hawsepipes by
hempen cables. But there was no magic in all
these sights and sounds to lighten the boy's
spirits. "The filial tenderness of his heart,"
says one of the earliest of his biographers, " at
first required a solace which it did not find."

His character, however, began to show itself
when Suckling arrived. The "Raisonnable" remained but a short time in commission, and
Suckling was appointed to a seventy-four-gun

ship called the " Triumph," stationed as a guard-ship in the Medway. The boy grew restless; he was seeing nothing of the sea life. How it came about I do not know that any of his bio-graphers explain; but whether through the advice of Captain Suckling, or because of the wishes of the Rev. Edmund Nelson, Horatio was sent on a voyage in a small ship to the West Indies. She was commanded by Mr. John Rathbone, who had served as master's mate under Captain Suckling. Nelson was absent in this voyage about a year. I confess, as one who has served under the red flag, that I love to think, and am honoured by thinking, of Nelson as a merchantman. The famous Cook was also a merchantman. Indeed, some of the finest seamen and greatest heroes of naval story have come out of our mercantile marine. But it is scarcely necessary to say this, seeing that the merchant service very greatly ante-dated the establishment of the Royal Navy. Even in Elizabeth's time one cannot think of Hawkins, Frobisher, Drake, and the many other stars of that splendid galaxy of sea chieftains, as Queen's men in the sense that a Royal Naval officer is now a Queen's man. They were buccaneers; the merchants found them ships; the Cinque Ports and the longshore yielded them crews who were composed of merchant sailors. The Navy grew out of the mercantile marine, and glorious as is the white flag, not less honourable is the red, whether for its memories of heroic combat or for its faithful discharge of the duties of that peace whose victories are not less renowned than war's.

Life in the merchant service last century was certainly harder than life in the Royal Navy. The ships went full of men, and the forecastles were small. They were not only small, they were foul, under-deck, loathsome dungeons. They were leaky; in head seas the water drained in and the seamen's chests floated about. A slush lamp would yield no light; a lanthorn with a candle in it merely made darkness visible. The merchant sailor was infamously fed. The humane " scientist" never dreamt of casting his eyes in the direction of Jack's caboose. Captain Cook worked a miracle by cleanliness and by never losing an opportunity of obtaining fresh provisions and vegetables. On the other hand, how it fared with the crews under Anson, who, though a bold and gallant officer, needed certain qualities eminently to fit him for the high trust of that expedition, may be read in the narrative of his voyage. The crews of the whole squadron had amounted to upwards of twelve hundred. Within one year of leaving England only three hundred and thirty-five remained alive. This fearful mortality was nearly wholly due to the scurvy.

It was not to be supposed that little Nelson lived in the forecastle of Rathbone's ship. No doubt he slept aft in the cabin, and ate with the captain. Rathbone probably laid in a few sea delicacies. One reads in old yarns of the captain of a frigate sitting down to a breakfast of coffee and toast and potted beef and tongue sliced *à la* Vauxhall. Rathbone would doubtless keep his weather eye lifting in these matters; but we may take it that Nelson also ate the food of the merchant sailor, — his brine-hardened pork, beef which you could tease with thumb and forefinger as though it were oakum you picked; pease soup which gave you a clear view of the peas at the bottom of the nauseous draught, and "duff" formed of dark flour and the greasy scum floating on top of the coppers. Therefore, so to speak, the lad shared in the sailors' mess-kid and drank of their scuttle-butt. Also he went aloft with the Jacks, helped reef, to light over to windward and to haul out to leeward, and he may have assisted in furling a royal or topgallant sail.

They needed full crews in those days, for everything worked like "drawing teeth." The sheave jammed on its pin — they had no patent trusses — the yards came round slowly. All hands would be wanted time after time, and Nelson pulled and hauled with the rest. One recalls a passage in a naval novel published five years after the death of Nelson: "The lieutenant went on deck. 'Mr. Echo,' said he to a midshipman, 'send the after-guard aft here to hoist the main-topsail.' 'Ay, ay, Sir!' cried Mr. Echo, who, in concert with half-a-dozen other weekly account gentlemen, thus vociferated for several minutes at the break of the quarter-deck — 'Boatswain's Mate! Boatswain's Mate! I say, you Boatswain's Mate! Send the after-guard aft here to the main-topsail halliards. Corporal of Marines! Send the marines aft on the quarter-deck to clap on the main-topsail halliards. Master at Arms! Go down below, and send all the idlers up! Send all the idlers up! Do you hear there, Master at Arms? Send all the idlers up! Stewards and servants, barbers and sweeps, cook's mates, and cook's mates' ministers, doctor's mates and loblolly boys! After-Guard! I don't see the After-Guard coming aft! Where's the Captain of the After-Guard! Pass the word, there, in the waist for the Captain of the After-Guard!"

Nelson returned from this voyage to the West Indies a thorough sailor. He had brought with him a forecastle growl of those days: "Aft the more honour, forward the better man." And he was not far wrong. He was bronzed, and he had broadened. He had picked up a thorough knowledge of practical seamanship. In a man-of-war in reefing he would have sat on the cap and yelled to the men; in Rathbone's ship he lay out on the yards and helped the seamen. He lived with the crew of this vessel during an impressionable period of his life; and there is little doubt that the sympathy he felt with sailors and his kind usage of them in after days, insomuch that he was more beloved by his crews than any captain or admiral I can find record of, was largely due to this voyage in a merchantman. Indeed, it is impossible to live with merchant seamen of a good sort, to share their privations, to lead their lives, to sit and yarn with them by the hour, and not part from their companionship without regret. The sentiment of the shipmate comes to you, and a habit of affection with the old life and the hearts you were thrown with will long survive your withdrawal from the career.

Many writers have expressed wonder that young Nelson should have returned from this voyage hating the Navy. He himself owns that he hated it, but speaks regretfully of the passing feeling. But his star of glory had climbed high in the heavens when he made this admission. He could easily have explained the real reason. In Rathbone's ship he enjoyed a liberty and freedom which were new sensations to him after the taut discipline of a man-of-war. He did not then consider that the Navy offered him any promise of reward for zeal and dutifulness. He beheld in Rathbone a melancholy instance of what he might consider the country's ingratitude. Here was a man who had served the State to the utmost of his ability for some years, and who, finding that he was no longer needed, had returned for his daily bread to the service which he had quitted for a man-of-war. Then, again, young Nelson knew that at the end of a merchantman's voyage the sailor lined his pocket with good money and was a free man. Happily for our country, these thoughts did not long possess him. Only think of Horatio Nelson, master mariner, never reaching anything higher in the sea-life than the command, perhaps, of a small West Indiaman!

CHAPTER II

"I WILL BE A HERO"

PICTURES of the life of Nelson fall into groups at this period of his career. I am of those who do not place much faith in the traditionary stories told of him. You read that he said to his grandmother when she expressed wonder that fear did not drive him home, "Fear never came near him." He robbed a pear-tree, not because he desired the fruit, but because his youthful comrades were afraid to begin. Such yarns might be told of anybody. His biographers carried their enthusiasm too far, and tried to find something remarkable and even preternatural in the most commonplace sayings and in the most insignificant actions of the boy. The old novelists had this trick. When they brought their heroes into the world they contrived that something amazing attended them, — a comet, a dream.

It is said that Nelson was but indifferently educated as a lad. But how much knowledge

is a boy of twelve going to carry to sea with
him? I knew one who went to sea at the age
of thirteen, and all the Latin and Greek he
possessed went irrecoverably overboard the first
night down Channel. This will be found true
of most lads who go to sea, where they cease to
read books because no books are there, and
where all is hard work, high seas, and the occa-
sional blessed relief of a spell below.

Nelson, as we have seen, returned from his
voyage from the West Indies with a hatred for
the Navy. " It was many weeks," he says,
" before I got in the least reconciled to a man-
of-war, so deep was the prejudice rooted; and
what pains were taken to instil this erroneous
principle in a young mind!" Captain Suckling
was no doubt astonished at first; he would then
be much amused at the little chap's forecastle
scorn of the noblest of all the callings. There
is a picture to be made here by representing
Nelson as one of the crew of the cutter and the
decked long-boat of the " Triumph." By this
means he became an adroit pilot in the navigation of the Thames and Medway. He says
that the two boats went as far as the North
Foreland. No doubt young Nelson was put to
heaving the lead. Suckling seems to have been
cordially desirous that the lad should turn out a

good sailor and an efficient officer; in fact, he
had sanctioned the boy's going in the boats on
condition that, to quote Nelson's words, "he
attended to his navigation." An old-world
scene of river and Channel rises in a vision before the mind's eye when one thinks of Nelson
in that long-boat sounding through the Nore,
through the Oaze Deep, past the dangerous
Girdler, then slanting away south for Margate
Sand until the great shoulder of the Foreland is
abreast and the green waters of the Channel
sparkle to the Downs. How quaint to our
eyes would be the ships of all sorts heeling
from the breeze! Yonder a cutter with a pen-
non as long as her hawser; nearer, an English
East Indiaman with high poop and stooping
bows, and a grin of artillery in her weather-worn
sides. Observe as she leans that her bottom
is unsheathed; the bright copper that was to
shed a glare as of sunset upon the brine that
creams along her side to windward and that
added a delicate grace to the taller, shapelier, and
statelier fabrics of later years, is seldom to be
heard of in the merchant service at this date.
Mark that round shape; she is floating past
Nelson's boat under wings of canvas stretched
by yards as square as those of a thousand-ton
ship of to-day. Her burthen is one hundred

and eighty tons; she is a snow-bound to Lisbon. Passengers are on board of her, and the women come to the side to look at Nelson's boat as their little ship floats past. Not very many years before, such another craft as this carried the famous Henry Fielding across seas to his grave.

The navigation of the mouths of the Thames and Medway was heavily charged with peril of a dark night, when the lanterns were few, if any, and when they certainly did not sparkle as they now do. To Henry Taylor, an old sea-captain of North Shields, do we owe the first floating light that warned the mariner to beware of that deadliest of shoals, the Goodwin Sands. Even when Nelson had achieved greatness, and was lying in his frigate off Deal watching the French, the seaboard was almost lampless. Small wonder that those should have been the days of ambling in sailing ships. In these times the first anxiety of the commander is to sight the familiar light. Then there was no light to make; so a man hove his ship to if he was at all doubtful, mixed a second glass of grog, lighted a pipe, and smoked with philosophic submission to the maritime conditions of the period. One objection the Trinity House raised to beaconing the Goodwin Sands was curious.

The Brethren were of opinion " That a light would be of advantage to privateers, who might be so audacious as to attempt to cut vessels out of the Downs, for it would direct them through the Gull-stream." How frivolous and contemptible, interpreted by the experiences of after years, are the objections urged against progress !

In this manner was Nelson employed until an application from the Royal Society induced the Government to equip and despatch a couple of vessels on a polar voyage. The ships were the " Racehorse," Captain Phipps, and the " Carcass," in charge of Captain Lutwidge. Nelson, at his own urgent request, was entered as a midshipman on board the " Carcass." He was probably haunted by curious imaginations of the North Pole and the North-West Passage. The mariner still continues to look for the North Pole, and it may be that before these lines are published he will have found it. The benefit of its discovery to mankind, however, the sailor has never yet attempted to explain. From the trembling stars of the West Indies to the white and death-like silence of the Polar regions was a wide range nicely calculated to test the constitution of a delicate young man. It seems to have done Nelson no harm. The voyage cer-

tainly enlarged his experience as a sailor. They
tell of him here that he wandered over the ice
armed with a gun in pursuit of a polar bear,
and when he was called to account for his rash-
ness, he answered, "Please, sir, I wanted the
skin for my father." There is nothing in this.
The young fellow's foolhardiness merely signified youth. It was not a characteristic. Possibly the anecdote is untrue — the invention of
early idolaters who have crowded his story with
melodramatic imaginations.

A voyage, however, into the bitter parallels
which were penetrated by the two ships would
certainly tend to harden a lad's power of endur-
ance. The "Carcass" was a bomb, as they
called it, a lubberly, motherly creation of the
yards of those days; something about three
times as long as she was broad, with full but-
tocks, and the run of an apple, and bows so
square that, as old seamen used to say, they
would drive an empty bottle a mile ahead with
them. That the ships were equipped as later
expeditions have been, will not be supposed.
We do not hear of preserved provisions in
those days, although canned meats were certainly in use at sea early in this century. If
Nelson was glad to go on this voyage, he was
doubtless equally glad to return. The cabin

accommodation must have been horrible; the hatches on for warmth, and the air below-decks in consequence pestilential, for the conundrum of ventilating a ship had not yet been solved. In the "Sketch" Nelson communicated to M'Arthur, he gives us a faint glimpse of his life in the far North: "When the boats were fitting out to quit the two ships blocked up in the ice, I exerted myself to have the command of a four-oared cutter raised upon, which was given me, with twelve men; and I prided myself in fancying I could navigate her better than any boat in the ship."

The two ships returned to England and paid off in October, 1773, on the 28th of which month one Mr. Kee, a Navy agent, received the following letter, delivered by young Nelson in person: "Mr. Bentham's Compliments to Mr. Kee; he understands he is Agent to Mr. Surridge, the Master of the 'Seahorse,' should be obliged to him for a recommendation in favour of Horatio Nelson, a young lad, nephew to Captain Suckling, who is going in that ship. The Master is a necessary man for a young lad to be introduced to, therefore Mr. Bentham will be obliged to Mr. Kee for a Letter. The ships wait only for the Commodore's despatches." Nelson was not yet fifteen years of age. His character is shown in his resolution to thrust forward. Not many other young fellows of his years in the Royal Navy would have rolled so swift and nimble an eye over the Service for opportunities as did young Nelson, and the first that offered he seized. He tells us: "I found that a Squadron was fitting out for the East Indies; and nothing less than such a distant voyage could in the least satisfy my desire of maritime knowledge." He was rated midshipman in his Britannic Majesty's ship "Seahorse," of twenty guns, commanded by Captain George Farmer; and he tells us that in this ship he visited almost every part of the East Indies, "from Bengal to Bussorah." We have no record that I am acquainted with, beyond Nelson's own bald statement, of his life, actions, and service at this period. The squadron was in command of Commodore Sir Edward Hughes, of whose kindness to him Nelson speaks gratefully. The climate of the East Indies proved too much: he fell ill, and Sir Edward sent him to England as midshipman in the "Dolphin," of twenty guns, commanded by Captain James Pigot, whose kindness, Nelson himself tells us, at that time saved his life.

If his earliest biographers are to be trusted, his ill-health during the passage home induced deep depression of mind.   He thought of himself as a plain country clergyman's son, a constant sufferer from ill-health, without influence to help him onwards.   This might very well be: so ardent and enthusiastic a temperament as Nelson's would know many moods and be visited by many impulses.   It is not hard to figure the poor young fellow leaning over the side of the "Dolphin," his eyes heedlessly following the foam-bells and the wreaths of cloud which swarmed through the blue brine to the white furrow at the rudder.   If his health should force him to quit the ocean, what was he to do?   But it is told of him by Clarke and M'Arthur that after many fits of crushing despondency, his heart delivered itself of its burden of gloom by help of this sort: "I felt impressed with an idea that I should never rise in my profession.   My mind was staggered with a view of the difficulties I had to surmount and the little interest I possessed.   I could discover no means of reaching the object of my ambition.   After a long, gloomy reverie, in which I almost wished myself overboard, a sudden flow of patriotism was kindled within me, and presented my King and country as my patrons.   My mind exulted in the idea. 'Well, then,' I exclaimed, 'I will be a hero,

and, confiding in Providence, I will brave every
danger ! "   I confess that a good deal of this
sounds very much as if it had been dictated by
Lady Hamilton to Harrison.   " I will be a
hero " !   There were few midshipmen in the
Service who did not want to be heroes, and
whether they confided in Providence or not,
they were always ready to cover themselves
with glory.   It is asserted, however, that Nelson would often afterwards declare to his friend
Hardy that from that hour there was suspended
before his mind's eye a radiant orb that courted
him onward to renown.

It will not be thought that Nelson at this
time was entirely without interest; for Captain
Suckling was now Comptroller of the Navy,
and his influence was considerable.   One seems
to find this in Nelson's own statement that
" This ship [the " Dolphin "] was paid off at
Woolwich on the 24th of September, 1776.
On the 26th I received an order from Sir James
Douglas, who commanded at Portsmouth, to
act as Lieutenant of the " Worcester " 64,
Captain Mark Robinson, who was ordered to
Gibraltar with a Convoy.   In this ship I was
at sea with Convoys till April 2nd, 1777, and
in very bad weather; but although my age
might have been sufficient cause for not en-

trusting me with the charge of a watch, yet Captain Robinson used to say 'he felt as easy when I was upon deck as any officer in the ship.'"

There was never a duty more thankless to the naval officer than that of convoying. His responsibilities were extremely heavy, and the insensibility of the merchant masters profoundly irritating. Ships of all sizes and different rigs would go away down Channel in a huddle, convoyed — in other words, protected — by perhaps a line-of-battle ship and frigates; but the strength of the men-of-war would depend upon the number of merchantmen they had to look after. It is difficult in this age to realise the audacity of the privateersman and the pirate in former years. These were gentry who, getting news of the sailing of a rich convoy, say to the West Indies, or, some of them, to the East, would hover upon the skirts of the crowd and cut one or another off, as a thief might sneak the loitering sheep of a flock. But in war-time a sterner danger was to be apprehended in the apparition of a squadron of the enemy's ships. The merchantmen then had to stagger off as best they could, leaving the men-of-war to engage the foe and cover their retreat or escape. No severer trial to the

temper did the naval officer experience than
the obligation of keeping a large body of merchantmen within the circle of the horizon.
Some would have a nimbler keel than others;
some were very dull sailers. While the courses
of some of the ships ahead might be dipping
in bland contempt of the signals of the men-of-
war, nothing but the royals and topgallant
sails of others would be visible astern. This
might be very well in the day; but when the
darkness closed in with squalls of wind, hard-
ening perhaps into dirty weather, what was the
naval officer to do? Happy was the commander who brought the whole of his sheep,
black and white, to their destination.

Nelson must have speedily got sick of this
work. Some fine sea pieces it doubtless presented. Think of a little timberman out of
the Gulf of Honduras climbing up the horizon
with dingy canvas and sweating head-boards,
and sailing into the midst of a convoy of a
hundred sail with frigates and other war-vessels
protecting them. The swarthy fellows leaning
over her side might imagine that the skipper
had lost his reckoning, and had carried them
into some vast, noble river of commerce full of
ships. This is among the vanished sights of
the world. In war-time will there be convoy-

ing in this age of steam? In any case the
naval commander will not labour under the
same difficulties which drew the language of
irritation, and often of profanity, from the
mouths of his predecessors. The propeller
will keep the steam-ships together, and the
liner of twenty knots will slow down to accom-
modate the tardy keel of the tramp of eight.

When young Nelson returned to England
he passed his examination at the Navy Office
as lieutenant. His commission was dated
April, 1777. He wrote to his brother William
jokingly: "I passed my Degree as Master of
Arts on the 9th instant." A copy of this
"Passing Certificate" from the Record in the
Tower is printed by Sir Harris Nicolas. Its
quaintness would alone make it interesting —

LIEUTENANT'S CERTIFICATES.   JUNE 1762.
MAY 1777.

"In pursuance &c., of the 5th April, 1777, we have
examined Mr. Horatio Nelson, who by certificate appears to be more than twenty years of age, and find he
has gone to sea more than six years in the Ships and
Qualities undermentioned (viz.)—

Raisonable	.. Mid.	..	..	0	5	0	1
Tryumph	.. Captain's Servant	..	..	1	2	0	2
"	.. Mid.	..	..	0	10	1	5
Carcass	.. Mid.	..	..	0	5	3	0

Triumph	.. Captain's Servant		..	0	0	1	5
Seahorse	.. Mid.	..	..	0	5	2	6
"	.. Able	..	..	1	7	1	6
"	.. Mid.	..	..	0	4	3	2
Dolphin	.. Mid.	..	..	0	6	3	6
				6	3	1	6

" He produceth journals kept by himself in the ' Carcass,' ' Seahorse,' ' Dolphin,' and ' Worcester,' and certificates from Captains Suckling, Lutwidge, Farmer, Pigott, and Robinson, of his diligence, &c.; he can splice, knot, reef a sail, &c., and is qualified to do the duty of an Able seaman and Midshipman. Dated the 9th April 1777. M.S., Captain John Campbell, Captain Abraham North."

When he went "up" for his examination Nelson is said to have entered the room in a very nervous state of mind. Nothing could be more likely; but the examination and the examiners were by all the measurement of the poles asunder not so stiff, harsh, needlessly oppressive as they now are. In this age an examination is a lofty hurdle designed to arrest the passage of the ingenuous youth of this country into independence and a profession. As an example of the tyranny of certain professional examiners I may state this of my own certain knowledge : the examiner asked a young man who was "trying for" the Army a question in history. It was correctly answered. "Are you sure you are right? Are you sure you are right?" cries the examiner hotly, with the hope of forcing him into a blunder. Could anything be more unfair? Nelson began nervously, but answered the questions correctly, and presently with spirit. Captain Suckling was present. He seems to have sat a silent spectator. When the ordeal was ended, he rose and introduced the youth to the examiners as his nephew. "Why did not you tell us this before?" was asked. "Because," was the answer, "I did not wish the youngster to be favoured. I felt convinced that he would pass a good examination, and, gentlemen, you see I have not been disappointed."

Next day Nelson was appointed to the "Lowestoffe," Captain William Locker. "A fine frigate of thirty-two guns," writes Nelson joyously to his brother William; "so I am now left in the world to shift for myself, which I hope I shall do so as to bring credit to myself and friends." His association with Captain Locker was the greatest stroke of good fortune that could have befallen him. Throughout his life he was never weary of recalling his obligations to Locker. This gallant officer had distinguished himself while first lieutenant of the "Experiment" by boarding and taking the French "Télémaque." He had served under Hawke. His fine qualities, his genial nature, are eloquent of the man in the kindly, round, sailorly face that looks at you from his print. "In this ship," says Nelson, speaking of the "Lowestoffe," "I went to Jamaica, but even a frigate was not sufficiently active for my mind, and I got into a schooner, tender to the 'Lowestoffe.'" This schooner was called the "Little Lucy," after a daughter of Captain Locker. In her Nelson went piloting, amid the intricacies of the Keys, to the north of San Domingo. I find but one noticeable incident in relation to his connection with the "Lowestoffe." The ship fell in with an American letter of marque. It was blowing fresh, and a high sea was running. The first lieutenant was ordered to go on board her. A boat was lowered, but the sea was so hollow that the lieutenant returned to the frigate professing his inability to get alongside the prize. Locker, much irritated, cried out, "Have I no officer in the ship who can board the prize?" The master ran to the gangway. Nelson stopped him. "It is my turn now," said he, "and if I come back it is yours." The story goes that a strong heave of sea carried Nelson and his boat's crew right over the American. He contrived to board her at last. Years afterwards he communicated this anecdote to the editors of the "Naval Chronicle." He wrote with pardonable self-complacency. "This little incident," he says, "has often occurred to my mind; and I know it is my disposition that difficulties and danger do but increase my desire of attempting them" — a statement which of itself, unsupported by the facts and acts of his life, must sufficiently refute the absurd opinion held by one or two that he was very wary and cautious, and without the brilliant dash and spirit which fascinated his contemporaries to hear of and charms us still to read about.

Nothing noticeable is to be found in Nelson's service under Sir Peter Parker. But he was shortly to enter a scene of excitement to himself, though the reader finds his doings a little colourless. He was about twenty years of age when he was appointed to the command of the "Badger," a small brig of war. From her he passed into the "Hinchinbroke." Whilst he was at sea news reached him of Count d'Estaing's attempting an attack on Jamaica with a very large fleet and army from Martinique. The rumour proved false. But Jamaica was filled with alarms and the batteries of Port

Royal were intrusted to the command of Nelson. He says proudly, " I need not say as the defence of this place was the key to the Port of the whole Naval force, the Town of Kingston and Spanish Town, it was the most important post in the whole island."

He is described at this period as having been very negligent in his dress. Perhaps he was always so. At this time he presented a figure that might have passed as an aforemast hand. One cannot wonder at this. He was drenched with the sea. He had sucked at her nipple till his blood ran in brine. He was blunt in speech, of a sailorly frankness of manner. At a little later date Prince William Henry, afterwards William IV., met and described him as the merest boy of a captain he had ever beheld. His dress, he said, was worthy of attention. His lank and powdered hair was tied in a stiff Hessian tail of an extraordinary length; and the grotesque appearance of the whole was heightened by the old-fashioned flaps of his waistcoat. The Prince stared at him. Never before had he met so singular a sailor. Lord Hood then introduced Nelson to the Prince, who was speedily captivated by his tact and conversation and by the enthusiasm which coloured and glowed in his references to his pro-

fession.   The naval officer in those days seems
to have enjoyed a wide license in the matter of
dress.   A story is told of Commodore Thomp-
son.   Clothed in a purser's duck frock and a
common straw hat, he passed in his boat under
the stern of the flag-ship.   The Admiral (Jervis) viewed the Commodore with amazement.
He then hailed the boat.   " Barge ahoy !   Go
and assist in towing that transport !"   This
rebuke may not have been relished.   It was,
however, understood.   The Commodore, singing out in the language of the salt, " Ay, ay,
Sir !" headed his barge for the transport and
helped to tow her.

The expedition to St. Juan formed an exciting period to Nelson.   But the narrative is a
little dull to readers.   The St. Juan expedition
was most unfortunately planned ;   the climate
was intolerable ;   the time, chosen with wonderful infelicity, was the rainy season ;   the plain of
war was a field of slime.   Men fell dead and were
loathsome with corruption before their comrades
had trudged out of sight of them.   Nelson was
nearly stung to death by a serpent.   He barely
escaped being poisoned through drinking at an
impure spring.   They ran short of food, and
made broth by boiling monkeys.   This delicacy
was too much for Nelson's stomach.   One

glimpse of the manly brutes simmering in the
coppers capsized him then and lastingly so far
as that particular sort of soup was concerned.
He toiled, however, with noble effort, undertook work without any obligation to do so, captured a battery at the head of a few seamen,
and was rewarded by Sir Peter Parker's offering
him the command of the " Janus," forty-four
guns. A reward indeed to a man nearly dead
of dysentery and fatigue !

He returned to Jamaica, where the ship then
was, but so ill that he was unable to move. He
was conveyed on shore in his cot to the lodging-
house of a black nurse called Cuba Cornwallis.
Sir Peter Parker took him to his own home
and nursed him as if he had been his son, but
to no purpose. There was no physic for the
young man but the climate of England, and
accordingly he sailed on September 4 in the
" Lion." On his arrival at Portsmouth he went
to Bath, and was treated by Dr. Woodward, a
well-known physician of that time. It seems
that in addition to his other ailments Nelson
was afflicted with the gout. Writing to Captain
Locker from Bath in January, 1781, he says :
" I have been so ill since I have been here that
I was obliged to be carried to and from bed
with the most excruciating tortures, but, thank

God, I am now upon the mending hand.   I am physicked three times a day, drink the waters three times, and bathe every other night, besides not drinking wine, which I think the worst of all."

Not long since I was looking at the lodgings in which Nelson lay ill. They are in Pierrepont Street, and the house was kept by one Mr. Spry. Always a gloomy street, I should think, falling into decay in this age, though in it when at Bath dwelt the Lord Chesterfield who was called by Johnson "a lord amongst wits, and a wit amongst lords." Dr. Woodward found Nelson a very good patient. In February, 1781 he was better, and had regained the use of his limbs except his left arm, which lay down his side as though it were paralysed. A pleasant story, told on the authority of Clarke and M'Arthur, is related of the physician who attended him. The doctor made a small charge. Nelson, surprised by the extreme moderateness of his fees, desired to increase them, on which Woodward said : " Pray, Captain Nelson, allow me to follow what I consider to be my professional duty. Your illness, Sir, has been brought on by serving your King and country, and, believe me, I love both too well to be able to receive any more."

CHAPTER III

IN August, 1781, Nelson found himself in command of the " Albemarle," a frigate of twenty-eight guns. He speaks with great pride of this appointment, and of his ship. He says she " has a bold entrance and clean run." Later on, in a letter to William Locker, he tells him that his ship is able to give the " Argo " (a new forty-four) the go-by.

There is something magical in the very word *frigate*. All the romance of the glorious Service enters her. Even then — but how much fairer in later days ! — she was a thing of beauty. Whether at anchor, with all her yards symmetrically braced, softly bowing to the south-east heave of sea in the Downs, or whether under full breasts, with courses climbing into milky heights of topgallant sail and royal, her sides brilliant with the lights of the deep and the day, here and there her decks spotted with the red coat of the marine, the frigate was ever to my mind the bravest and the most picturesque

of all the thunderous guardians of these coasts.
Marryat has described life on board of her.
But he could not paint a ship, he could not
tinge it with poetic colours, nor find in the
fabric a hint of the spirit of the Great Mother
whose spacious breast she walked.

One there was, however, who could — Michael Scott, the most masterful of them all in
marine revelation.   Here is a sketch by him,
and it might stand as a portrait of the " Albemarle," omitting only the " milk-white streak " :
" The press of canvas she was carrying laid her
over until her copper sheathing, clear as glass
and glancing like gold, was seen high above
the water throughout her whole length, above
which rose her glossy jet-black bends, sur-
mounted by a milk-white streak, broken at
regular intervals into eleven goodly ports, from
which the British cannon, ugly customers at
the best, were grinning, tompion out, open-
mouthed at us ; and above all the clean, well-
stowed, white hammocks filled the nettings
from tafferel to cathead.   Oh ! that I had been
in one of them, snug on the berth-deck !   Aloft,
a cloud of white sail swelled to the breeze till
the cloth seemed inclined to say good-bye to
the bolt-ropes, bending the masts like willow-
wands (as if the devil, determined to beat Paga-

nini himself, was preparing fiddle-sticks to play a spring with on the cracking and straining weather shrouds and backstays), and tearing her sharp wedge-like bows out of the bowels of the long swell, until the cutwater and ten yards of the keel next to it were hove clean out of the sea, into which she would descend again with a roaring plunge, burying everything up to the hawse-holes, and driving the brine into mist, over the foretop, like vapour from a waterfall, through which, as she rose again, the bright red copper on her bow flashed back the sunbeams in momentary rainbows."

I trust I shall be forgiven this lengthy extract; it is a sketch by one who lived closer to Nelson's time than we do, who wrote in years when the Nelson traditions and inspirations were the influence they had been in the time of Trafalgar. Not yet had the paddle-wheel been introduced to churn romance away astern. Small wonder that the seaman of old loved his ship. To him she was a thing of life. She could do everything but talk. He would have loved her better but for the Admiralty habit of shifting crews from one vessel to another. Nelson quarrelled with this short-sighted practice, knowing as a seaman that affection in a sailor is the flower of association.

I am not writing the life of Nelson : I am merely attempting to depict certain scenes of his splendid and devoted career. There is little, then, to talk about when we come to this passage of the " Albemarle." Again he was pestered by the convoy, and wrote : " Two hundred and sixty sail the convoy consisted of. They behaved as all convoys that ever I saw did : shamefully ill ; parting company every day." Before he and a portion of the ships he was looking after fetched Yarmouth Roads, a privateer was reported in the thick of the merchantmen. Nelson, in his frigate, gave chase, and rapidly overhauled the pirate, but after an hour's pursuit was obliged to return to the fleet, lest other sea-wolves should be among the clumsy craft. This pirate was a scoundrel named Fall. He commanded a cutter called the " Folkestone," and under French colours had fired upon several places on the coast of Scotland. It is interesting to think of Nelson chasing a pirate — of all the enemies of man the basest, the cruellest. " Give the privateersman the stem ! " used to be the old cry. Other foes deserved mercy at the hands of their British captors ; the pirate none.

One or two anecdotes of dramatic interest are related of Nelson in connection with this

cruise. When he was off the coast of North
America he captured an American fishing-
schooner belonging to Cape Cod. As he was
in want of a pilot he took the unfortunate
master of the schooner on board the frigate,
and the fellow served him very faithfully.
That plant of rare cultivation, gratitude — as
Dr. Johnson calls it — was one of the qualities
always in full bloom in the breast of the man
whose individuality was even then the most
fascinating afloat or ashore. When the poor
skipper had completed his work, Nelson called
him aft and said, " You have rendered us a
very essential service, and it is not the custom
of English seamen to be ungrateful. In the
name, therefore, and with the approbation of
the officers of this ship, I return your schooner,
and with it this certificate of your good conduct.
Farewell, and may God bless you." There is
a theatrical touch here, and many might suspect
the accuracy of this story in consequence of that
hysterical " God bless you." But Nelson was
essentially an emotional man, just the sort of
sailor out of the fulness of his heart to round
off the cordial phrase of gratulation with a
benediction. Anyway, there was long, and
there may yet be, in existence the certificate
which Nelson gave to Nathaniel Carver, master

of the schooner " Harmony," on Aug. 17, 1782.

It is told that whilst at Quebec Nelson fell in love with an American lady. He would have been no true sailor had he not been fond of the girls. Doubtless he had poured down many a glass of grog to that famous old forecastle pledge, " Here's the wind that blows, and the ship that goes, and the lass that loves a sailor!" The "Albemarle" was ready for sea when Alexander Davison, a great friend of Nelson, who was standing upon the beach, saw the young commander coming ashore in a boat. " What brings you back?" asked Davison. " I'll walk with you to your house," answered Nelson, "and explain matters. The fact is, Davison, I find it utterly impossible to leave this place without again waiting on her whose society has so much added to its charms, and laying myself and my fortunes at her feet." Davison bluntly told him that, situated as he was, such a step would ruin him. Nelson persisted. Davison probably exerted physical force. He may have passed his arm through his friend's, and, eloquent with entreaty, but always moving towards the sea, got him to enter his boat that was ashore. He watched Nelson rowing away to his frigate, and no doubt considered that in rescuing him from this marriage he had preserved a valuable life.

It does not seem that the image of the beautiful American lady long troubled him. She was not one of those shapes which "come not at an earthly call," and "will not depart when mortal voices bid." He was sent to the West Indies, but the fighting was over, and the "Albemarle" returned to England in June, 1783. He took a lodging in Salisbury Street, Strand, and devoted himself to the task of procuring the wages for his crew, whom with delightful sympathy he calls "my *good fellows*." Such was his popularity that when his ship was paid off, the whole of the men offered, if he could get another ship, to enter for her immediately. He seems, however, to have had no thought of going to sea just then. Living on board ship cost more than he could afford. Extravagance of living probably attended King George's entering his third son, Prince William, as midshipman in the Navy with the idea of popularising the Service. I do not know that this device made forecastle Jack much more numerous, though its object was this primarily; but it certainly filled the quarter-deck with nobs and snobs. A derisive story is told of a lieutenant of a man-of-war hailing the mizzen-topsail yard, and shouting : " My lords and gentlemen, and all you right honourable lubbers, bear a hand and roll up that sail and lay down ! " This influx of swells doubtless brought extravagance of living along with it, and Nelson, who had nothing but his pay to support him, remained ashore.

In October he applied for leave to visit France on " my private occasions." And early in November we find him dating a letter to William Locker at St. Omer. Nelson in France ! Nelson in that country whose foundations his thunders of the Nile and Trafalgar were to shake to their heart ! In after years " Down, down with the French ! " was his ceaseless cry. He sent William Locker a very diverting account of his journey. They left Dover at seven o'clock, put to sea with a fine north-west wind, and at half-past ten " we were safe at breakfast in Monsieur Grandsire's house at Calais." Nelson was much amused by the ridiculous figure of the postilions in their jackboots, and their rats of horses. He slept at Marquise on a straw bed, and supped off two pigeons served on a dirty cloth, with wooden-handled knives. At Montreuil he lodged in a house whose landlord had recommended Le Fleur to Sterne. The voyagers steered for St.

Omer, where they fell in with two naval captains, Ball and Sheppard. One was afterwards Rear-Admiral Sir Alexander John Ball, and Nelson's close friend. The other died Vice-Admiral of the Red. When Nelson saw them, he conceived a strong dislike to them both; they wore fine epaulettes, and he thought them great coxcombs for that. Nevertheless, a few years later — that is, in 1795 — epaulettes were ordered to be worn as part of the British naval uniform.

Nelson's own description of his travels into France, as addressed to his brother, is too good to be omitted. His style is quaint and old-fashioned. We see him here as an observer of other things than sea affairs : " On Tuesday morning, the 21st ult., I set off from Salisbury St. in company with Captain Macnamara of the Navy, an old messmate of mine. I dined with Captain Locker, my old Captain, at Malling in Kent, and spent the night at his house. The next day we slept at Dover, and on Thursday morning we left England with a fine wind. In three hours and twenty minutes we were at breakfast in Monsieur Grandsire's at Calais. The quick transition struck me much. The manners, houses and eating so very different to what we have in England. I had thoughts of

fixing at Montreuil, about sixty miles from
Calais, in the road to Paris. We set off *en
poste*, they called it; we did not get on more
than four miles an hour. Such *carriages*, such
horses, such *drivers*, and such *boots* you would
have been ready to burst with laughing at the
ridiculous figure they made together. The
roads were paved with stones; therefore by
the time we had travelled fifteen miles, we were
pretty well shook up, and heartily tired. We
stopped at an inn, *they called it* — a clean pig-
stye is far preferable. They showed us into a
dirty room with two straw beds: they were
clean; that was all they could brag of. However, after a good laugh we went to bed and
slept very soundly till morning. How different
to what we had found the day before at Dover!

"At daylight we set off, breakfasted at Boulogne, and got to Montreuil in the evening.
This day we passed through the finest country
my eyes ever beheld; not a spot (as big as my
hand) but was in the highest cultivation, finely
diversified with stately woods. Sometimes for
two miles together you would suppose you were
in a gentleman's park. The roads are mostly
planted on each side with trees, so that you
drive in almost a continual avenue, but amidst
such plenty they are poor indeed. Montreuil

is situated upon a small hill, in the middle of a
large plain, which extends as far as the eye can
reach, except towards the sea which is about
twelve miles from it. Game here was in the
greatest abundance ; partridges, pheasants, wood-
cocks, snipes, hare, etc., etc., as cheap as you
can possibly imagine. Partridges two pence
halfpenny a brace, a noble turkey fifteen pence
and everything else in proportion. You will
suppose that it was with great regret we turned
our backs upon such an agreeable place, but
not a man that understood English, which was
necessary to learn me French, could be found
in the place. Our landlord at the inn is the
same man that recommended Le Fleur to Sterne.
From this place we proceeded on to Abbeville,
ninety miles from Calais. This was a large
town, well fortified, but even there I could not
be accommodated to my wish : nor indeed good
masters, that is, that understood grammatically.
At last I determined to come here, which
indeed is what we ought to have done at first,
therefore by the time we arrived here, which
was Tuesday week, we had travelled a hundred
and fifty miles, but upon the whole I was not
displeased with our excursion. This is by
much the pleasantest and cleanest Town I have
seen in France. It is very strongly fortified,

and a large garrison. We had good rooms in a pleasant French family, where are two very agreeable young ladies, one of whom is so polite as to make our breakfast for us, and generally when we are at home, drink tea and spend the evening with us. I exert myself, you will suppose, in the French language, that I may have the pleasure of talking to them; and French ladies make full as much use of their tongues as our English ones. We have a most pleasant society of English at this place. We have seldom a day but we are invited somewhere, which I avoid as much as possible that I may acquire the French, and there are three families that I visit *en famille;* that visiting pleases me far beyond the other. My paper is done: in my next I shall proceed; I have much to say. To-day I dine with an English clergyman, a Mr. Andrews, who has two very beautiful young ladies, daughters. I must take care of my heart, I assure you."

Nelson began to learn French. He made slow progress. He made quicker progress in love. He met, as we see by his letter, the daughters of an English clergyman named Andrews, and lost his heart to one of them. The memory of the American beauty went out of his head. "She has such accomplishments," he

says, speaking of the girl, "that had I a million
of money I am sure I should at this moment
make her an offer of them; my income at present is by far too small to think of marriage, and
she has no fortune." Love mastered him, for
here was a greater conqueror even than Nelson.
What broadside equals in fatefulness the arch
and sparkling glance of a beautiful woman's
eyes? Nelson hauled down his flag, but that
was all he could do; the girl declined to take
possession of the prize whose colours he had
struck to her.

How perfectly human, genial, tender; how in
full touch with all human sympathy was the
noble nature of this glorious little man, may be
seen in his letter to his uncle William Suckling,
dated Jan. 14, 1784. He sets out with a solemn countenance; he is axiomatic: "There
arrives in general a time in a man's life (who
has friends) that either they place him in life in
a situation that makes his application for anything farther totally unnecessary or give him
help in a pecuniary way if they can afford and
he deserves it." And then he tells Suckling that
he is in love. The critical moment of his life
has arrived; he is to be happy or miserable —
it depends solely on Suckling. His income,
Nelson points out, does not exceed one hundred

and thirty pounds a year. Miss Andrews has but one thousand pounds to her fortune, and she and Horatio can't live upon that. Will Suckling, then, make him a yearly allowance of one hundred pounds until he has increased his own income to that extent? He winds up in the well-known language of the fond shepherd: "I am prepared to hear your refusal, and have fixed my resolution if that should happen; but in every situation I shall be a well-wisher to you and your family, and pray they or you may never know the pangs which at this instant tear my heart." To think of Mr. Suckling, of the Customs, with his heart torn by pangs of love!

Needless to say, Nelson did not marry the lady. His liberal uncle would have acceded to his wishes, but the lady declined. This was Nelson's one defeat, but it happened ashore, and must not find a place in the list of his battles.

On March 19, 1784, he wrote to his brother, who was now the Reverend William Nelson, that on the preceding day he was appointed to the command of the "Boreas" frigate. The ship was full of young midshipmen, and his treatment of them is but another example of his sweet and noble character. It does not seem, however, that his midshipmen were always as grateful to him as they should have proved

He tells in his own rough way to William Locker, whilst he lies in the Downs, the story of an un-grateful midshipman, whose name, I gather from Harris, is sunk in oblivion. It will be seen by his letter that captains of ships had other anx-ieties than fighting them and commanding them *only*.

" I need not say it to you, but what in the *name* of *God* could it be to me whether a Mid-shipman in my Ship had not a farthing or fifty pounds a year? Therefore, now I must tell you, as far as I know, his wish to leave the ship. When he came on board I sent him into Mr. Bromwich's mess, where he was two or three days. In that time they spoke to me, that they hoped I would not take it amiss, but they could not think of keeping that young man (I forget his name) in their mess, as he could not pay his part in their small expenses. I am sure that you will not think I should attempt to force any person upon people who were behaving exceed-ingly well in the Ship (which would have been *tyrannical* in the highest degree) against their inclination. Whether the lad sent to speak to me, or I sent for him, I do not recollect, but I told him of what the mess had said. He then seemed very uneasy at what I told him, and said he could not afford to live in a mess that cost anything, and then said he wished to leave the ship. The next day he pressed me much to discharge him, as he could not live in any of the mid-messes. Much against my inclination I did *discharge* him. What he took the idea of £30 a year from, I know not; for I declare I never opened my lips to him upon the subject. A youngster in the Ship, whose friends are Norfolk people, who had not made an allowance for their son, I took upon me to allow £20 a year.

" I assure you I hold myself under very great obligations to you, that you asserted it was an *infamous lie !* Had I in the least suspected the story he has told, he should have stayed on board and might have lived as he pleased. It was my endeavouring to put him in a comfortable situation that has made any person speak ill of me. If he had come into the ship as many hundred youngsters of the kind do, and the Captain had (*a word illegible*) to him, or of him to anybody for . . . months, I should have had no trouble about him."

Some of the lads of the " Boreas " were afraid to climb the masts, and, let me say, if you are constitutionally nervous, the task of climbing the rigging, straining, like a fly on the ceiling, over the futtock shrouds into the top, thence to

the cross-trees, upwards to the giddy height of
the royal yard, is painful and distressing. The
horizon has opened into boundlessness, the
large surge has dwindled into a ripple, the figures moving upon the decks are pigmies; the
sails fall from you in swelling rounds of fleece-
like clouds filled with the thunder and the music
of the wind. There you are perched close to
heaven; the melodies of the rigging might be
the quiring of the opening skies; but how to
get down? Nelson quite understood all this,
and to encourage the timorous among the midshipmen gazing with dread aloft, he would say:
"I am going a race to the masthead, and beg
I may meet you there," then would spring into
the lee-shrouds, while the nervous younkers
squeezed the tar out of the weather-rigging.
When they met in the top he would hearten the
lads with cheerful speech and say: "How much
any person was to be pitied who could fancy
there was any danger or even anything disagreeable in the attempt!"

Can you wonder that this man should have
been beloved by his officers and crew? Moreover, he was studious, at the cost of all personal
inconvenience, to set a good example. He was
always first to arrive on deck at noon to take an
observation. Every day he would enter the

school-room of the frigate and listen and watch while the lads worked. This we have on the authority of Lady Hughes. He was carrying her Ladyship and her daughter to the West Indies. Lady Hughes was the wife of Admiral Sir Richard Hughes, of whom, after his arrival, Nelson would think and write with contempt and aversion as Commander-in-Chief. Lady Hughes he equally disliked. He could not know the sympathy and intelligence with which she was observing him during the passage. With Nelson also went his brother, the Rev. William, as chaplain. This person makes a very disagreeable figure upon the Nelsonian stage, and the more one reads about him the less one likes him. He was a born cadger, sleek, insincere, clamorous with professions when something was to be got, a round man in a square hole. The character of his old father stands high beside his; though every one must wonder that a clergyman should sanction such an association as that of Lord Nelson with Lady Hamilton by expressing willingness to dwell under the woman's roof. The worst that one can say of old Edmund Nelson is that he was a bore; he carried the clerical habit of sermonising people who stood in no need of his admonitions, to a degree that must often have set

Nelson's teeth on edge. The Rev. William, sick of the sea and stung by mosquitoes, left the ship shortly after her arrival.

Loyalty and dutifulness rendered Nelson's life a very uneasy one in this period of his career. The Americans had ceased to be colonists, and our Navigation Laws forbade the foreigner from trading in British possessions. When Nelson came upon the scene he found that a very large illegal traffic was being carried on, and, to his disgust, he discovered that Sir Richard Hughes, faithlessly indifferent to British interests, was secretly conniving at what was going forward. Nelson forthwith went to work to suppress all this wrong-doing. He captured many vessels. It will not be supposed that his zeal was much appreciated. He retorted with a saying worthy of some great admiral or general of Cromwell — that men-of-war were sent abroad for other purposes than to be made a show of. He recommended the indignant Sir Richard Hughes to study the Navigation Acts. Sir Thomas Shirley, Governor of the Leeward Islands, a beef-faced man with a liver enriched by draughts of sangaree, blustered out to Nelson that, " By God, Sah ! old generals are not in the habit of taking advice from young gentlemen, Sah !"

" I am as old as the Prime Minister of England," answered Nelson, contemptuously, " and think myself as capable of commanding one of his Majesty's ships as that Minister is of governing the State."

But we will pass from this dry record of Navigation Acts and contraband Yankees to a passage of pure romance. The beautiful American had been one; Miss Andrews had been another; and now in a third he was to meet his fate. When he was at the Island of Nevis he went ashore to dine at the house of a Mr. Herbert, who was then President of the island. At the table sat a lady who seemed to find something very curious and interesting in the little captain of the " Boreas." She watched him attentively, and when she went home she wrote an amusing account of him to Mrs. Nisbet, a great friend of hers then at St. Kitts. Little did this good and critical young woman foresee the issue her underlined and chatty letter was all unconsciously shaping.

Who was this lady's great friend, Mrs. Fanny Nisbet? She was niece of the Mr. Herbert with whom Nelson dined: a widow with one child; her husband, Josiah Nisbet, had died mad eighteen months after his marriage. To Mrs. Nisbet the critical lady who had sat at dinner with Nelson described how the little captain came up just before the meal was ready, much heated; he was very silent, though he seemed to think the more. He drank no wine till the toasts of the King, the Queen, the Royal Family, and Lord Hood were given, and then " this strange man," continues Mrs. Nisbet's correspondent, " regularly filled his glass and observed that those were always bumper toasts with him." After he had passed the bottle he sank into silence. The lady's critical inspection of him became a sort of trouble to her. She must have stared very hard, and if she was not pretty Nelson might not have felt flattered. She tells her correspondent that she was very much puzzled; she could not make out the little man's real character. His demeanour was stern and reserved, but she noticed that when he spoke he always said something worth attention. " If you, Fanny, had been there you would have made something of him; for you have been in the habit of attending to these odd sort of people."

Not many months later this " odd sort of person," as the lady would have termed him, was writing thus at seven in the evening to Mrs. Fanny Nisbet: " As you begin to know something about sailors, have you not often heard that salt water and absence always wash away love? Now, I am such a heretic as not to believe that Faith, for, behold, every morning since my arrival I have had six pails of salt water at daylight poured upon my head, and instead of finding what the seamen say to be true, I perceive the contrary effect; and if it goes on so contrary to the prescription you must see me before my fixed time. At first I bore absence tolerably, but now it is almost insupportable, and by and by I expect it will be quite so."

He was head over ears in love; he had met the young widow at Nevis, and found her very pretty, young, of a most engaging disposition, and very cultivated. His letters to her show all the warmth of a devoted lover. The apologists of Nelson's connection with Lady Hamilton represented Fanny Nisbet, afterwards Lady Nelson, as cold, wanting in tact and in sympathy with her husband's noble profession. But *he* had to wait until he met Lady Hamilton to find this out.

He wrote to his uncle, William Suckling, asking for pecuniary help, — in short, the gift of a thousand pounds. Suckling appears to have behaved kindly, for Nelson wrote to his

Fanny, March 3; 1786: " From my uncle Suckling I have a very kind letter, saying he will do every thing in his power to add to my happiness; and if I should want it, that he will give me pecuniary assistance." Then, again, there was Fanny's uncle, Mr. Herbert, a very rich man as wealth went in those days — his negroes and plantation stock were valued at sixty thousand pounds. Of this gentleman Nelson wrote as follows to Suckling: " But I must describe Herbert to you, that you may know exactly how I stand; for when we apply for advice, we must tell all circumstances. Herbert is very rich and very proud — he has an only daughter, and this niece, who (*sic*) he looks upon in the same light, if not higher. I have lived at his house when at Nevis, since June last, and am a great favorite of his. I have told him that I am as poor as Job; but he tells me he likes me, and I am descended from a good family, which his pride likes; but he also says, ' Nelson, I am proud, and I must live like myself, therefore I can't do much in my lifetime: when I die she shall have twenty thousand pounds; and if my daughter dies before me she shall possess the major part of my property. I intend going to England in 1787 and remaining there my life; therefore if you two can live happily together till that event takes place you have my consent.' This is exactly my situation with him; and I know the way to get to him to give me most, is not to appear to want it: thus circumstanced, who can I apply to but you?"

A striking and characteristic anecdote is related of Nelson at this time. One day, while the " Boreas " was lying at anchor in Nevis Road, a French frigate passed to leeward, close along shore. It reached Nelson's ears that the object of the frigate's presence in those waters was to survey the British West India Islands, for which purpose she had on board two general officers and some engineers. Nelson at once weighed and gave chase. He found her next day at anchor in the Road of St. Eustatia, and he anchored his frigate about two cables' lengths on the Frenchman's quarter. There was much civility, of course: mutual salutes, bows, and grimaces; and then the Dutch Governor invited Nelson and his officers to meet the French officers at dinner. They met; the scene is full of humour to an English reader, for you are quite sure of the way in which a sea affair will be worked out when Nelson has the handling of it and when he is

dealing with Frenchmen. The conversation
was brisk, the wine went the rounds; then
Nelson spoke. "I understand, Sir," he said
in effect, addressing the French commander,
"that it is your intention to visit the English
islands, and, this being so, I consider it my
duty to accompany you in my frigate that attention may be paid to the officers of his most
Christian Majesty, which I am sure every
Englishman in the islands will be proud of an
opportunity of doing." The offer was by no
means relished by the French officers, who,
with all contortions of native politeness, begged
to be excused from Nelson's attendance, as their
intention was merely to cruise round the islands
without stopping at any one of them. Nelson,
however, was not to be outdone in civility, and
his ship continued to ride hard by the French
frigate. His drift could not be mistaken. In
a few days the Frenchmen abandoned their
project, got under way, and beat up to Martinique. Nelson beat up to Barbadoes, thus
contriving to keep the Frenchman in sight
until he reached the island he had come from.
He refers to this thorough "Nelson touch"
in a letter to Mrs. Nisbet : " For the last week
a French man-of-war has been here [he means
in West Indian waters], and going about with

them so much in the sun has given me violent headaches."

Nelson married Fanny Nisbet March 12, 1787. The "Pegasus," in command of Prince William Henry, was on that station at this time under Nelson, and the Prince had expressed his desire to be present at the marriage, that he might give the bride away. This he did, and very naturally Nelson felt himself extremely honoured. The Prince was unquestionably a sincere admirer of Nelson. He seems to have expounded him with a prophetic gaze. The relations of the two in the West Indies make pleasant reading: on the Prince's part all was sailorly sympathy, kindness without condescension, with just so much of reserve as should distinguish his exalted position and make his friend easy by perception that the character of his friendship was nicely understood; while, on Nelson's, all was good taste and tact, everywhere self-respect and dignity strongly coloured by loyalty; in short, not a hint of snobbishness. His character greatly rises in one's esteem in the perusal of this intercourse.

Fanny's maiden name had been Woolward. She was born about 1763, and was some twenty-four years old when she married Nelson. A month after this marriage the "Boreas" was

found to be rotten; and Nelson, writing from
Antigua to the Admiralty, says, "that if the
ship does not reach England before the hurricane season, she will be too bad for the voyage."
She reached Spithead July 4, 1787, but Mrs.
Nelson made the voyage home in a merchantman. Hard times were now at hand for Nelson. His means were small. He could not
obtain employment. It was some months after
her arrival before the "Boreas" was paid off.
And Nelson complains that he was as much
divorced from his wife as if he had remained in
the West Indies. The frigate lay at the Nore,
and sometimes seven miles from the land, so
says Nelson, on impress service. It is declared
that Nelson felt his neglect so keenly that had
he possessed an independency he never would
have gone to sea again. Sir Harris Nicolas
finds no foundation for this in his "Correspondence." Professor Laughton is also very posi-
tive. "There is absolutely no reason," he says,
"to give the slightest credence to the story that,
in his extreme disgust, he determined to throw
up his commission and quit the service." To
judge by this writer, not only what the hero did,
but what he thought, must be strictly in correspondence with admiralty requirements. Long
subsequent to this date Nelson wrote that he

was a man, and that he could not help *feeling* as a man.   No one was more sensitive to neglect; no man of genius more thoroughly understood his own powers and possibilities.   He had done great work for the country in the West Indies, and for some years he was to remain without employment.   Would not the ardent soul of such a man fret?   But does it not fret in that "Correspondence" which Nicholas himself edited?   How does Nelson write, for instance, on May 6, 1788?   "You have given up all the toils and anxieties of business, whilst I must still buffet the waves — in search of what?   That thing called Honour is now, alas! thought of no more.   My integrity cannot be mended, I hope, but my fortune, God knows, has grown worse for the Service: so much for serving my country."   Again, it is sad to find him writing in September, 1789 : "Not being a man of fortune is a crime which I cannot get over, and therefore none of the Great care about me.   I am now commencing Farmer, — not a very large one, you will conceive, but enough for amusement.   Shoot I cannot, therefore I have not taken out a license ; but notwithstanding the neglect I have met with, I am happy, and now I see the propriety of not having built my hopes on such sandy foundations as the friendships of the Great." And again it is sad to find him in June, 1790, writing to the Duke of Clarence: "My not being appointed to a ship is so very mortifying that I cannot find words to express what I feel on the occasion; and when I reflect on your Royal Highness's condescension in mentioning me to Lord Chatham, I am the more hurt and surprised. Sure I am, that I have ever been a zealous and faithful Servant, and never intentionally have committed any errors; especially as till very lately I have been honoured by the notice of the Admiralty."

In a note in the "Despatches and Letters," Nicolas, basing his remarks upon the information of Clarke and M'Arthur, states that the "Boreas" payed off early in the summer of 1787. Nelson had received several rebukes or reprimands from the Admiralty; his correspondence respecting frauds in the Public Departments had been coldly received; he had incurred great anxiety and exposed himself to heavy responsibility in supporting the commercial interest of his country, and on his return to England the "Boreas" was made a receiving ship for impressed seamen at the Nore. This treatment is stated to have so irritated his mind that he said to the senior officer in the River

Medway : " I now rejoice at the ' Boreas ' being ordered to be paid off, which will release me for ever from an ungrateful Service, as it is my firm and unalterable determination never again to set my foot on board a King's Ship. Immediately after my arrival in Town I shall wait on the First Lord of the Admiralty and resign my Commission." A resolution which was happily prevented by his receiving a very civil letter from Lord Howe, desiring to see him in town. The interview proved satisfactory to both parties, and Lord Howe offered to present him to the King at the next Levee, when he was honoured with a gracious reception.

There is no more painful reading than Nelson's applications for a ship. He asks for the " Raisonnable," his first sea-home ; nay, it is asserted, and Nicolas scarcely denies, that he begged command of even a cock-boat. He went to live with his wife at Burnham Thorpe. His irritable spirit throbs like a pulse of fever in the picture of his life at this time. There could be no repose when Nelson is unemployed and ashore. But little of the truly rural spirit enters into the account his biographers give of his killing the time by digging in his father's garden, hunting for birds'-nests with his wife, shooting

with a gun, but so awkwardly that his piece
was a menace to the lives of everything but the
object he aimed at.   They tell us he was fond
of coursing.   He mused upon charts, read the
current prints, drew plans.   One day he went
to the fair to buy a pony.   Whilst he was
absent, two rough fellows arrived at the Par-
sonage and asked for Captain Nelson.   Mrs.
Nelson informed them that he was out, where-
upon they handed her a writ on the part of the
American captains, who laid their damages at
many thousands.   Nelson's sensations on his
return may be imagined.   He is reported to
have exclaimed : " If the Government will not
support me, I will leave the country."   It is
even declared that he wrote to the Treasury
and threatened that if a satisfactory answer were
not sent him by return of post he would take
refuge in France.   He was to go first; and
Mrs. Nelson was to follow, ten days later, under
the care of his elder brother, Maurice.   If this
is a lie, it is very circumstantially related by
those whom Nicolas frequently quotes.

War gave him his chance, but not till the
early months of 1793.   On January 7 in that
year, Lord Chatham, with apologies for neglect,
offered him the command of a sixty-four gun-
ship, and on January 30 he was appointed to

the "Agamemnon."   "*Post nubila Phœbus!*"
he wrote to his wife, "after clouds comes sunshine. The Admiralty so smile upon me that
really I am as much surprised as when they
frowned."

CHAPTER IV

ST. VINCENT

ON the forenoon of the 11th of February, 1797, two British frigates, the "Minerve" and "Romulus," were lying at anchor off the then new mole in the Bay of Gibraltar. At Algeciras floated three Spanish line-of-battle ships. The wind blew a fresh breeze from the east, and it was a fine morning.

Presently the "Minerve," which flew a Commodore's broad pennant at her mast-head, got under way. There was never a fairer sight than the picture of a British frigate getting her anchor and flashing into canvas. As if by magic she was clothed from waterway to royal yard-arm, and heeling from the breeze and under command of the helm, while a foreigner would be leisurely sheeting home his topsails, and getting into a mess forward with his jib sheets to windward.

No sooner had the "Minerve" started than two of the three Spanish line-of-battle ships were observed to be in motion. In short, it was speedily seen that they intended to chase the British frigate.   Spain had declared war against Great Britain and was in coalition with France, and she had sent forth upon those seas which she never could command a flotilla designed to annihilate that ancient foe, whose merchant seamen, led by buccaneering chieftains, had swept her Armada up Channel into the North Sea, and so left it to struggle round about to its own destruction.

On the quarter-deck of the " Minerve " two persons were walking.   One was Commodore Nelson, whose broad pennant was at the masthead ; the other was Colonel Drinkwater, afterwards Bethune.   Since Nelson's appointment to the " Agamemnon " he had seen a good deal of service ; he had fought in a not very glorious battle with the French, thanks to the withering prudence of Hotham, the Admiral in command of the British ; he had lost the sight of an eye in Corsica ; in many directions had he been active.   He was now sailing to join the fleet under Admiral Sir John Jervis, doubtless to be met with somewhere in the waters off Cape St. Vincent.   The Spanish line-of-battle ships brought the steady east wind along with them ; the " Minerve," on the other hand, was for some time bothered by the eddies and baffling

flaws which you get near the Rock when the
wind is east. But presently she took the
breeze full and fair, and slanted along with
fairly nimble French heels; for French she
was by birth, having been captured in the
Mediterranean in 1795.

When it was discovered that the Spaniards
were after her, the frigate was cleared for action.
Her situation was critical, even though Nelson
was on board. Two huge line-of-battle ships
opposed to a little frigate! Colonel Drinkwater said to Nelson as they walked the deck
together, that there seemed every probability
of the enemy overhauling and engaging the
"Minerve." "An engagement is quite possible," answered Nelson. "The headmost ship
appears to be a good sailer. But," he added,
looking up at his broad pennant, "before the
Dons get hold of that bit of bunting I will
have a struggle with them, and sooner than
give up the frigate, I 'll run her ashore." Here
the Captain of the frigate (Cockburn) who had
been viewing the chasing enemy through a
spy-glass, stepped up and said that he believed
the headmost ship was gaining upon them.
This conjecture did not hinder the company
from going below to dinner, which was just
then announced. Before Nelson quitted the

deck the order was given to set studding-sails.
At table Colonel Drinkwater was seated next
to Lieutenant Hardy (the " Kiss me, Hardy ! "
of the " Victory's " cock-pit, always a favourite
of Nelson) ; he had fallen into the hands of the
Spaniard, and had recently been exchanged.
The Colonel was offering him his congratulations when the dreadful cry of " Man overboard ! " echoed into the cabin through open
skylight and companion-way.   The ship's officers rushed on deck.   Drinkwater ran to the
stern windows to see if the unfortunate man
was in sight.   Instead of the man, he saw one
of the frigate's boats with a party of sailors, and
Hardy at the helm.   The current of the Strait
set strongly eastward, and soon the boat was
far astern of the " Minerve."   Apparently the
man had sunk on striking the water — he was
never seen again.

Hardy speedily signalled that the man was
lost, and his crew put all their weight of British
muscle into their oars to regain the frigate.
What an extraordinary situation ! — a boat full
of men struggling against the deadly set of the
current, and beyond her the snow-white towers
of the huge Spaniards sharpening upon the eye
into distinctness as they drove the brine boiling
from them with metalled forefoot !   Nelson,

casting one look at the boat and another at the enemy, cried out, " By God, I 'll not lose Hardy ! Back the mizzen-topsail." This was done, the frigate's way was arrested, and the brave hearts astern, with redoubled exertion, drove their clumsy boat through the snarl of sea.

Now how would a novelist rescue the British frigate from this situation of extraordinary peril ? Would he dare invent the escape that really happened ? Perhaps it would not have happened but for the terror excited by the name of Nelson, even *then*, albeit the mighty tragedies of St. Vincent, the Nile, Copenhagen, and Trafalgar were yet to be enacted. It was known by the Spaniards that Nelson was on board the " Minerve." The foremost of the pursuers on seeing the frigate bring her mizzen-topsail to the mast believed that she meant to fight. Let it be credited, to employ the expression of Drinkwater, that the captain of a Spanish ship of the line did not consider himself an equal match for a British frigate with Nelson on board ! The Don shortened sail to allow her lubberly consort to join her. This stratagem of fear enabled the " Minerve" to drop down to her boat, and having picked up Hardy and his crew, she proceeded on her voyage under a press. By sunset both the hulking Spaniards were out of sight.

Amongst the passengers in the " Minerve " was Sir Gilbert Elliot, the Viceroy of Corsica, by whose side, in a cot in the frigate's after-cabin, slept Colonel Drinkwater. On the night following the alarms of the day the Colonel was awakened by the opening of the cabin door; a light was burning in the fore-cabin. He observed some person enter, and after peering, made out by the dim light that it was Nelson.

" Is Sir Gilbert awake ? " Nelson asked.

" No," answered the Colonel ; " has anything fresh happened ? "

Nelson stepped to his cot, and said in a low voice, he had every reason to believe that the " Minerve " was at that very moment in the midst of the Spanish Fleet. Their signals assured him it was not Sir John Jervis's.

" The night is foggy," continued Nelson. " The ' Minerve ' is now between two very large ships, within hail of each of them ; others are close aboard on all sides. Neither Cockburn nor I have the least doubt that the strangers are Spanish."

" This is out of the frying-pan into the fire," said the Colonel, who was clearly now very wide awake, though the Viceroy continued to snore.

" We have certainly got into something like a scrape," said Nelson. " It is quite unavoidable on account of the night and the fog. With address we may extricate ourselves. If they are not the Spanish Grand Fleet, they may be a convoy or a detached squadron proceeding to the West Indies, and destined to strengthen the Spanish naval force in that quarter. If so, it is of the first moment that the British commander on the West Indian Station should be early apprised of these movements of the enemy. This duty I shall undertake instead of joining Sir John Jervis."

The Colonel listened with consternation. The idea of being conveyed to the West Indies was horrible. He hoped to find a means of escape in the Viceroy.

" What will you do with Sir Gilbert Elliot? " he asked. " It is of the greatest importance that he should not only see Sir John Jervis, but reach England with the least possible delay."

Nelson answered: " I 'll go on deck and see how things are there."

Sir Gilbert still snored, and the Colonel was considerate enough not to waken him, though he was aroused afterwards by a second visit from Nelson. The " Minerve " was so manœuvred as to seem to belong to the ships. As they wore or tacked so did she, contriving, nevertheless, to edge away insensibly. Thus she managed to scrape clear of what actually proved to be the Spanish Grand Fleet.   Nelson shaped a course which he believed would give him a sight of the ships of the night, and settle his doubts one way or the other.   But, in spite of a bright lookout, nothing hove into view, until at daybreak on the 13th of February, when, in the haze of the dawn, a brig and a cutter were sighted, and soon after a larger sail, which proved to be the British frigate " Lively," an outskirt of Sir John Jervis's fleet.

The curtain now rises upon one of the most majestic sea-pieces on record.   A battle was to be fought, and the British Admiral, Sir John Jervis, was overheard to say to himself, " A victory is very essential to England at this moment."   Public alarm in this country was great indeed.   We feared that the Spaniards would effect a junction with the French and sweep the Channel from Land's End to the South Foreland.   Colonel Drinkwater declares that " nothing but England's disgrace and downfall was foretold and talked of throughout the kingdom." It was even coming to the closing of the Bank of England and the general suspension of cash payments.   In these times of peace, which all must hope will long continue,—in spite of the old West Indian naval toast, " A bloody war and a sickly season " [1] — it is hard to realise the very uneasy lives led by people who dwelt in the towns on our coast. Families visit Ramsgate or Brighton nowadays, and not the least idea of a line of French and Spanish ironclads bombarding their apartments disturbs the enjoyment with which they view the children sporting in the surf or digging in the sand. Very different was it a hundred years ago. The spy-glass of the longshoreman ceaselessly swept the line of the horizon in search of the topmost cloths of the gigantic enemy who hoped to shake these kingdoms to their foundation. Indeed, down to 1805, the scare of invasions, of huge floating armaments, was continual. Not a hundred years ago ! Has the demon of steam worked such a change that our longshore panics never can recur ? Let us hope it has.

On falling in with the British Fleet, Nelson at once went on board the " Victory," Jervis's flag-ship, and on the same afternoon shifted his broad pennant to the " Captain." The Spaniards were not far off. Nelson was able to report this for certain, and before sunset on the evening of the day preceding the fight, the signal had been made for the British ships to

[1] Quoted by Lieutenant Parsons in his " Nelsonian Reminiscences."

prepare for battle. Throughout the hours of darkness the vessels kept in close order. There is something wonderfully impressive in the picture of those fifteen towering giantesses whitening the dusk of the night with a light of glimmering canvas, moving slowly, stately, grimly onwards, a hush upon the decks, little to be heard but the sob of the sea at each thrust of cut-water. The human expectation in them, the hopes but not the fears, gave them a sentience of their own; they moved like lofty goddesses, instinct with the spirit of the high and splendid hearts that crowded them.

The preparation for battle was not then as it now is. Cutlasses were ground, pikes sharpened, pistols flinted: these were for the boarders. They filled powder and fitted well-oiled gun locks to the great cannon, and slung their lower yards with chains. One who was present in that memorable battle says that the Signal-Lieutenant called from the main yard of the "Barfleur," peering into the haze, "I have a glimpse through the fog of their leeward line, and they loom like Beachy Head. By my soul, they are thumpers! for I distinctly make out four tiers of ports in one of them, bearing an Admiral's flag." "Don Cordova in the 'San-

tissima Trinidad,"' says Vice-Admiral Walde-
grave, "and I trust in Providence that we shall
reduce this mountain into a molehill before
sunset."

Whilst this was passing aboard the "Barfleur," the gallant Jervis was walking the quarter-deck of the "Victory." "Make the signal
to prepare for battle," said he. How all that
is noble, heroic, gallant, dashing, in the long and
glorious sea-story of our country leaps to our
appreciation with the mere utterance of the
name of Jervis! As he walked, the hostile
numbers were reported to him as they appeared
by signal. "There are eight sail of the line,
Sir John." "Very well, sir." "There are
twenty-five sail of the line." "Very well, sir."
"There are twenty-seven sail, Sir John," and
this was accompanied, says my authority, a
Quarterly Reviewer, by some remark on the
great disparity of the forces, Jervis's fleet consisting of fifteen sail of the line only. "Enough,
sir! No more of that!" exclaimed Jervis. "The
die is cast; and if there were fifty sail I would
go through them."

The Spanish foe was a splendid but a formidable sight. He floated in mountains grinning
with artillery. The "Santissima Trinidad" sat
like a cathedral in her enormous bulk of timber,

pierced by the teeth of a hundred and thirty-six guns. She was believed to be the largest ship in the world. Unfortunately, in our day somebody has discovered that she was not a four-decker, and so another harmless tradition nods to its fall to the blast of old Dryasdust's blunderbuss. James describes the vessel as having been built at Havana in the year 1769, as a one hundred and twelve gun-ship, similar to the " San Josef" or " Salvador del Mundo " except probably in possessing rather more breadth of beam. It appears that some time between the commencement of 1793 and the end of 1796, her quarter-deck and forecastle were formed into a whole deck, barricades built up along her gangways, and ports cut through them, so as to make the total number of eight-pounders on that deck equal in amount to the twelves on the deck next below it. This accounts for one hundred and twenty guns: the remaining four, we may suppose, were mounted on the poop. The " Santissima Trinidad " was therefore a flush four-decker, that exceeded the three-deck one hundred and twelves in force only by fourteen eight-pounders and four pieces of a still smaller calibre. It was immediately noticeable that the Spaniards, however formidable they looked, were making a very ill figure in a tactical sense. Parsons, who, as an eye-witness, I am willing to quote, says: "They made the most awkward attempt to form their line of battle. And they looked a complete forest huddled together." Jervis formed his fleet in line-of-battle, and headed so as to cut off some of the Spanish ships to leeward. Several Spanish line-of-battle ships and frigates, separated from their main body, stood away on the starboard tack, aimlessly firing as they went. The leading British ship was the "Culloden," commanded by Troubridge, one of the finest and bravest of the sea officers of that day of marine giants. As she floated into the wake of the Spaniards the signal was made to tack in succession, and the "Culloden" instantly put her helm hard down. There are plenty who have passed their opinions freely on the subject of this signal. There can be no doubt, however, that the signal to tack in succession was an error of judgment. Such a strategy would oblige every British ship to arrive at the point where the ship immediately ahead of her had tacked before shifting her helm for the signalled manœuvre, and this would give the Spaniards plenty of time to go clear of their foe and either put themselves into a proper posture of battle or sail right away for home. It was Nelson who, observing the blunder flying

at the "Victory's" mast-head, determined not
to heed it, and, with the instincts of a consum-
mate seaman and the perception of a born
tactician, he put his helm up and headed for
the "Santissima Trinidad." The mighty Spaniard was compelled to put his helm down.
This gave time to Troubridge and other headmost ships to arrive. Nelson's bold and decisive manœuvre was a breach of discipline, a
defiance of Jervis. It is an illustration, however, of his amazing spirit and impetuosity of
character. He saw what was the right thing
to do, and did it without giving an instant's
thought as to what the consequences might
prove to him, — not, indeed, if his one ship
should be defeated and silenced by her gigantic
opponents, but if Sir John Jervis, the tautest
of disciplinarians, should deal with him afterwards. He might, perhaps, have guessed he
had nothing to fear on this score. Jervis
loved him. After the battle, Captain Calder
said something to Jervis in depreciation of
Nelson. Jervis, as we shall presently see,
would not listen to him.

Let us now attend to the proceedings of
Nelson. Having wore ship, as we have seen,
he passed between the "Diadem" and the
"Excellent," and was speedily engaged with

the leewardmost of the Spanish division. He was in the thick of the "Santissima Trinidad," the "San Josef" and "Salvador del Mundo," both of one hundred and twelve guns, the "San Nicolas," and two other first-rates. Sir Gilbert Elliot and Colonel Drinkwater, watching, on board the frigate "Lively," this marvellous sight of one comparatively small British ship engaged with a cluster of towering Spaniards, naturally expected to see Nelson annihilated. Indeed, they thought his conduct extraordinary and unaccountable. He was presently supported by the "Culloden," Captain Troubridge, but for some time these two vessels were fighting the most unequal battle on record. The iron hurricanes of the Spaniards had almost wrecked the "Captain" aloft. At last arrived the "Blenheim," which passing to windward of them, and ahead, to use Nelson's phrase, "eased us a little." The "Salvador del Mundo" and "San Isidro" had dropped astern, and were compelled by Collingwood's passing broadsides to hoist English colours. Collingwood was in command of the "Excellent." He and Nelson were old and affectionate friends. They had served together in the West Indies, and by a strange chance, which had something of destiny in it, when we think that these two men came

together at Trafalgar again, the ships which
Nelson had commanded in the West Indies
had proved so many links in the promotion of
the career of Collingwood.

The " Excellent," having delivered her smash-
ing broadsides, held on for the support of Nelson, whose situation was certainly very critical.
To use the language of Nelson, Collingwood
disdained the parade of taking possession of
beaten enemies, and " most gallantly pushed
up to save his old friend and messmate." The
" Captain's " plight was little less than that of
the sheer hulk's. She had lost her fore-topmast.
Every sail had been shot away. Every shroud
and rope was an end. And the wheel was
gone. She could prove of no further service
in the line or in chase. The " Excellent "
ranged up with every sail set, and passing
within ten feet of the " San Nicolas," the ship
that Nelson was fighting, poured into her one
of Collingwood's most awful and tremendous
drenches. The wretched Spaniard luffed, and
the " San Josef " fell on board her. That cool,
austere, and wonderful seaman, Collingwood,
then passed on for the " Santissima Trinidad "
at the time when Nelson ordered his helm to
be shifted, and called for the boarders.

There were some soldiers of the 69th on

board, and headed by their lieutenant (Pierson) they were the first to make the attempt to board the huge "San Nicolas" of eighty-four guns. Boarding was always the toughest of the many tough and grim duties of the seamen of those days. A very small swell of sea would suffice to keep the two flaming antagonists reeling and parting, reeling and parting in regular pendulum tick. By the boarding-pike was the prowess of our country established, and her greatness maintained, not in the capture of line-of-battle ships, but in marvellous cutting-out expeditions and in single-ship actions. The ironclad has removed a deadly weapon from the hands of the Jacks; but let not the enemy exult, for if the pike has foundered the heart is still afloat, and the heart must always be first.

The earliest to gain the "San Nicolas's" mizzen-channel was Berry, the First Lieutenant of the "Captain." A soldier broke open the upper quarter gallery window, leapt, and was followed by Nelson and others. The cabin doors were fastened, and the Spanish officers fired down through the skylights with pistols. But one broken door sufficed to liberate the boarders, the soldiers fired a volley, and the Spanish Commodore fell. Nelson rushed on to the quarter-deck, and found Berry in posses-

sion of the poop, and the Spanish ensign hauling down.   The ship was in their possession.
But another trouble was alongside, for just then
the " San Josef" began to fire muskets and
pistols from the Admiral's stern gallery.   Nothing was to be done but board her, and so seize
and silence her.   Little risk attended this.
Scarcely had Nelson entered her main chains
when a Spanish officer, looking over the quarter-deck rail, exclaimed that the ship had
surrendered.

Possibly this was the most thrilling moment
in Nelson's life.   Two line-of-battle ships captured by boarding !   Even after the battle is
over and Nelson sits down and muses, he seems
unable to realise it all.   " The more I think of
our late action," he wrote to his wife, " the
more I am astonished; it absolutely appears a
dream."   And he writes to Sir Gilbert Elliot :
" To receive the swords of the vanquished on
the quarter-deck of a Spanish first-rate can
seldom fall to the good fortune of any man."
Memorable and wonderful is that picture of
the wrecked British man-of-war lying alongside
her two huge prizes, with Nelson on the quarter-
deck of one of them, receiving from the Spanish
Captain, who bends his knee, the honourable
sword of a man who had done his best and

could do no more. He said that the Spanish
Admiral was dying of his wounds below. Nelson gave him his hand, and requested him to
inform his officers and the ship's company that
the vessel had surrendered. This he did.
" And," says Nelson, " on the quarter-deck of
a Spanish first-rate, extravagant as the story
may seem, did I receive the swords of the vanquished Spaniards, which, as I received, I gave
to William Fearney, one of my bargemen."

The flag-ship, the " Victory," in sailing past
the amazing marine triplet, thrice cheered with
lungs of storm, and when Nelson afterwards
went on board this ship to see the Admiral,
Jervis received him on the quarter-deck, em-
braced him, and thanked him again and again
in fifty kind expressions for his magnificent
services. The Battle of St. Vincent was really
won by Nelson. There is no doubt but for
his prompt and extraordinary measure the
meeting of the fleets would have ended in little
more than a futile distant cannonading. The
Spaniard would probably have withdrawn to his
port, and awaited another opportunity for putting himself into a more powerful posture of
defence by junction with the Frenchmen at
Toulon. How high and generous is the heart
of the seaman ! All will admit that Colling-

wood bore a large part in Nelson's achievement on this glorious Valentine's Day. Yet with what modesty does he refer to his share! " My dear good friend," he writes, on the day following the battle, " first let me congratulate you on the success of yesterday, on the brilliancy it attached to the British Navy, and the humility it must cause to its enemies; and then let me congratulate my dear Commodore on the distinguished part which he ever takes when the honour and interests of his country are at stake. It added very much to the satisfaction which I felt in thumping the Spaniards that I released you a little. The highest rewards are due to you and 'Culloden.' You formed the plan of attack, we were only accessories to the Dons' ruin, for had they got on the other tack they would have been sooner joined, and the business would have been less complete;" and he signs himself, " I am ever, my dear friend, affectionately yours, C. COLLINGWOOD."

Small wonder that the great novelist, Thackeray, should have found something to almost reverentially admire in this simple-hearted, modest, noble-minded sea-warrior! How tender was the regard of those sailors for one another! How unaffected their enthusiastic admiration for the heroic qualities, and how superb is the diffidence everywhere manifested! They fight as only Englishmen do fight at sea, and then, with the sweat and reek of the battle still upon them, they sit down and write affectionate congratulatory letters one to another, and they write home cheerfully to their wives, and send their blessings to their children, and every syllable that falls from their lips or their pen glows and lives with manly loyalty and devotion to the throne and the country they love.

Nelson's own account of the battle in a letter to his brother, to whom he naturally opens his heart more freely than to strangers, is worth reading : —

"Many thanks for your kind letter of March 13th, and I beg you will thank all our friends for their kind congratulations; and I must be delighted when, from the King to the Peasant, all are willing to do me honour. But I will partake of nothing but what shall include Collingwood and Troubridge. We are the only three Ships who made great exertions on that glorious day : the others did their duty, and some not exactly to my satisfaction. We ought to have had the 'Santissima Trinidad' and the 'Soberano,' seventy-four. They belonged to us by conquest, and only wanted some good fellow to get alongside them, and they were ours.

But it is well; and for that reason only we do not like to say much.

"Sir John Jervis is not quite contented, but says nothing publicly. An anecdote in the Action is honourable to the Admiral, and to Troubridge and myself. Calder said, 'Sir, the "Captain" and "Culloden" are separated from the Fleet and unsupported; shall we recall them?' 'I will not have them recalled. I put my faith in those ships; it's a disgrace that they are not supported and separated.'" [I break into Nelson's narrative with this anecdote from Tucker's "Life of St. Vincent." He says that in the evening, while talking over the events of the day, Captain Calder hinted that the spontaneous manœuvre which carried those *duo fulmina belli* Nelson and Collingwood into the brunt of battle, was an unauthorised departure by the Commodore from the prescribed mode of attack. "It certainly *was* so," replied Sir John Jervis, "and *if* ever you commit such a breach of your orders, I will forgive you also."] "You will not be surprised to hear I have declined all hereditary Honours; and as to entailing a Title, unless you have a good estate to send with it, you send misery; and till I became a Flag-officer, I had not made both ends meet. Chains and Medals are what no fortune and connexion in England can obtain; and I shall feel prouder of those than all the Titles in the King's power to bestow."

I limit myself in this reference to the battle of St. Vincent to Nelson's share in it. It would carry me beyond the purpose of these contributions to describe the battle at large, — nor, indeed, does the relation of a conflict at sea make very entertaining reading. Nothing is more insipid than to hear that at fourteen seconds past nine, H. M. S. "Noah's Ark" hauled up her courses and fired her larboard bow gun at the enemy. We need a large general canvas, a gorgeous Turneresque confusion, volumes of white powder-smoke scarlet with the lancing flash, the crash of the falling spar, the yells of the wounded, the cheers of the victors. One must always regret, however, that the "Santissima Trinidad" made good her escape. We hear, indeed, of her again at Trafalgar, where, of course, she is properly accounted for. But so noble a heap of frowning timber would, of them all, have most gallantly graced that British conquest. Nelson's rewards consisted of the freedom of the city of London in a gold casket, and a sword of honour. The freedom of the city of Norwich was also conferred. The King made him a Knight of the Bath. He was promoted rear-admiral, though it seems that this recognition was not owing to his claims as a conquering hero.

After the battle Nelson went on board the frigate " Lively," where he found Colonel Drinkwater, who reported some interesting conversation with him.

" Where is Sir Gilbert ? " was his first inquiry.

" Gone with Lord Garlies to the ' Victory,' " was the Colonel's reply.

" I hoped," he rejoined, " to have caught him before he saw the Admiral ; but come below with me," and he led the way to the cabin.

" How came you, Commodore, to get into that singular and perilous situation ? "

" I 'll tell you how it happened.   The Admiral's intention, I saw, was to cut off the detached squadron of eight sail, and afterwards attack the main body, weakened by this separation.   Observing, however, as our squadron advanced, and became engaged with the enemy's ships, that the main body of the enemy were pushing to join their friends to leeward, by passing in the rear of our squadron, I thought, unless by some prompt and extraordinary measure the main body could be diverted from this course, until Sir John (at that time in action in the ' Victory ') could see their plan, his well arranged designs on the enemy would be frustrated. I therefore ordered the 'Captain' to wear, and passing the rear of our squadron, directed Captain Miller to steer for the centre of the enemy's fleet, where was their Admiral-in-Chief seconded by two or three deckers, hoping by this proceeding to confound them, and, if possible, make them change their course (as he did), and thus afford Sir John Jervis time to see their movements, and take measures to follow up his original intention.

" I saw," he continued (and then he spoke with increased animation), " that from the disabled state of the 'Captain' [his ship] and the effective attack of the approaching British ships, I was likely to have my beaten opponent taken from me : I therefore decided to board the ' St. Nicholas,' which I had chiefly fought, and considered to be my prize. Orders were given to lay the ' Captain ' aboard of her ; the spritsail-yard passed into her mizzen rigging. Lieutenant Berry with the ship's boarders, and Captain Pearson with the sixty-ninth regiment (acting as marines on board the ' Captain '), soon got possession of the enemy's ship. Assisted by one of the sailors, I got from the fore-chains into the quarter-gallery through the window, and thence through the cabin to the quarter-deck, where I found my gallant friends already triumphant."

"The Admiral," observed the Colonel, " of course will be made a peer, and his seconds in command noticed accordingly. As for you, Commodore," continued the Colonel, " they will make you a baronet."

The word was scarcely uttered, when, placing his hand on the Colonel's arm, and looking him most expressively in the face, he said, —

" No, no ; if they want to mark my services it must not be in that manner — "

" Oh ! you wish to be made a Knight of the Bath," for Drinkwater could not imagine that his ambition at that time led him to expect a peerage. His suppositions proved to be correct, for he instantly answered, —

" Yes, if my services have been of any value, let them be noticed in a way that the public may know me — or them."

It is explained by this that he regarded a baronetcy as too costly, and that he wished to bear about his person some honorary distinction to attract the public eye and mark his professional services.

" Joy sparkles in every eye, and desponding Britain draws back her sable veil and smiles," wrote turgid old Edmund Nelson to his son.

Lady Nelson's letter was more to the point:
"Yesterday I received your Letter of February
16th. Thank God you are well, and Josiah.
My anxiety was far beyond my powers of expression. M. Nelson and Captain Locker behaved humanely and attentively to me. They
wrote immediately, Captain Locker assuring me
you were perfectly well, Maurice begging me
not to believe idle reports, the 'Gazette' saying you were slightly wounded. Altogether,
my dearest husband, my sufferings were great.
Lady Saumarez [whose husband, Captain Sir
James Saumarez, commanded the 'Orion' in
the Battle] came running to tell me she had
letters from her husband — all this was on this
day week. He speaks generously and manly
about you, and concluded by saying 'Commodore Nelson's conduct is above praise.' You
were universally the subject of conversation. . . .
I shall not be myself till I hear from you again.
What can I attempt to say to you about Boarding? You have been most wonderfully protected; you have done desperate actions enough.
Now may I — indeed I do — beg that you
never Board again. *Leave* it for *Captains*. How
rejoiced Jo. [meaning her son, Josiah Nisbet]
must have been to have seen you, although it
was but an absence of two months. To-morrow

is our wedding day, when it gave me a dear husband, my child the best of fathers. I hope he will deserve all the blessings Providence has bestowed on him. . . . Do come home this summer, or in the autumn. It is said a change in Administration would certainly have taken place had not this wonderful and fortunate Victory taken place. Admiral Parker, it seems, had written the 'Captain' and 'Culloden' bore the brunt of the Action. This instant have I received a letter from Lord Hood, telling me Sir Robert Calder was gone to Portsmouth. Thank you, my dearest husband, a thousand times for your letter of February 22nd. God bless and protect you, and my Joe! — crown all your endeavours with success, and grant us a happy meeting. I can bear all my extreme good fortune. Your affectionate Wife, Frances H. Nelson."

CHAPTER V

AFTER the battle of St. Vincent, Nelson, whose broad pennant was flying aboard the " Irresistible," went upon one of the most romantic of all the cruises a man could be despatched on. He, with a small squadron, was to look out for and fall in with, if possible, three Spanish ships of the line with an immense treasure on board. Also on board of one of them was the Viceroy of Mexico. The name of the treasure-ship, the plate-ship, the ship deep with minted money and ecclesiastical furniture in precious metal, fills the imagination with the colossal figure of the galleon. She was the dream of the buccaneer, the darling of Drake's heart; for her Anson defied the horrors of the Horn. It did not signify that the ships which Nelson was searching for were line-of-battle ships much after the pattern of the " Victory" and the " Culloden"; they had treasure aboard, and all the romance of the old galleon, with her castellated stern and her very flowing sheets,

comes into them with that.   One may say with
Wordsworth, —

"It is not now as it hath been of yore."

If a lading of treasure freighted the full-
breasted hull of the galleon with the amplest
and most gorgeous spirit of romance, how should
it be with us in these days when, if you glance
at the money article in your newspaper, you will
see that one, two, say three steamers, great mail-
liners, are in one day expected home with such
wealth of minted gold aboard as makes the rich-
est of the old galleons cut but a very sorry
figure?   And whereas those old galleons were
shoving, gold and silver laden, through the
broad ocean once in a blue moon for old Spain,
in our time every day finds its twenty galleons
on the sea, some rushing east, some darting south
and west ; fabrics which in the night pass through
the shadow in bodies of light, which in the day
are such goodly sights for their leaning chimneys,
their frothing race, the flash of glass, the rainbow
at the stem, the twinkle of uniforms, the gay
raiment of women, that no Englishman clearly
understanding that they are all born (and their
souls in the shape of engines given to them) in
this fair country but will own to a thrill of pride
as he watches them.

Nelson met neither with the Viceroy nor with the treasure. While he cruised his gallant ship the "Captain" was refitting, and when he made an end of his search he once more shifted his pennant to his old valorous craft. It is noticeable throughout this time that he was writing in language of the deepest affection to his wife — noticeable, I say, because, unhappily, the Syren is waiting for him round the corner, and their second meeting, preordained by that Providence which shapes our ends, was not to be very long delayed.

He was haunted by a dream of a cottage — it is the sailor's dream — a cottage not necessarily by the sea ; nay, planted rather in a fertile and plenteous country, which burnishes the autumn with its harvest, and fills the year's early months with the delicious concerts of the woods. Those who hold Nelson to have been ambitious will find no such quality in this passage of his life. His expectations, even though St. Vincent had been fought and he was the hero of whom everybody was talking at home, rose no higher than a little cottage. This, for instance, is how he writes to his wife in June 1797 : " Rest assured of my most perfect love, affection, and esteem for your person and character, which the more I see of the world the more I must admire. The imperious call of honour to serve my country is the only thing which keeps me a moment from you, and a hope that by staying a little longer it may enable you to enjoy those little luxuries which you so highly merit. I pray God it may soon be peace, and that we may get into the cottage."

Does a man write like this to a cold, unsympathetic wife? Even in the Teneriffe business, which we are shortly to catch a glimpse of, his last thought before going ashore was for his wife. He called young Nisbet, his step-son, into his cabin to help him to arrange and burn his mother's letters. On perceiving that Josiah was armed, he begged him to remain behind, saying, " Should we both fall, what will become of your poor mother? And the care of the 'Theseus' falls to you; stay, therefore, and take charge of her." Nisbet answered spunkily : " The ship must take care of herself. I'll go with you to-night, if I never go again." That's how it was, then, with Nelson in his relations with his wife, and it is a thing good to remember and pleasant to repeat.

News reached Jervis one day that a rich Spanish ship, bound from Manila to Spain, was lying at Santa Cruz. Jervis, now Earl of St. Vincent, conferred with Nelson as to an attack on Tene-

riffe and the seizure of the treasure-ship. Three
ships of the line and three frigates were sent on
this service. Nelson, whose flag was on board
the " Theseus," foresaw many difficulties. He
had previously suggested to Jervis an attack on
Teneriffe, but then he had relied on the assistance of troops. This is truly a melancholy
passage in the life of Lord Nelson. Who that
has ever beheld that mighty ocean "pike" of
Teneriffe, and watched the rollers foaming round
the granite rock, but must realise the prodigious
risk which Nelson and his men were about to
encounter, not only in the dominating forts and
an alarmed and furious population, but in the
giant forces of Nature herself, — rugged declivi-
ties, the spite of off-shore squalls, and the savage
trouble of hollow seas ? Nelson himself wrote
the story : he chose a Friday on which to embark one thousand men, including two hundred
and fifty marines, the whole commanded by
Captain Troubridge. Friday never yet was a
good day for the seaman, and it never will be.
Wind and tide belated the frigates ; the dark
night which was to have witnessed the attack
paled into dawn and discovered the British to
the Spaniards. "Thus foiled in my original
plan," says Nelson, " I considered it for the
honour of our King and country not to give

over the attempt to possess ourselves of the town, that our enemies might be convinced there is nothing which Englishmen are not equal to."

At eleven o'clock on the night of July 24, boats containing between six and seven hundred men, and a cutter called the " Fox," full of sailors, plied oars through the dusk towards the town. The sea was working; the wind blew with weight and an edge. Nelson was in one of the boats, and all were hoping that a landing might be effected before the Spaniards saw them coming. Suddenly the night was flashed up with the fire of thirty or forty pieces of cannon and musketry. The whole sea-front of the town had opened upon the British, but nothing could arrest those resolute oarsmen and captains. A shot plunged into the " Fox" cutter and sank her out of hand; a great shriek went up, but still, through the darkness and through the broken waters, those boats filled with British hearts moved slowly onwards. But a dreadful misfortune was now to happen; a large proportion of the boats failed to see the Mole, and went on shore through what Nelson described as " a raging surf." Every boat was stove: those who came off with their lives stormed the Mole, though opposed by five hundred men, captured it and spiked the guns. But nothing was to be done in the face of the heavy fire of musketry and grape-shot poured into the British from the citadel and houses at the head of the Mole. "We could not advance," says Nelson, "and we were nearly all killed or wounded."

Shortly after leaving his boat, Nelson's right arm was almost shot off. He cried out, " I am shot through the arm! I am a dead man!" His step-son, Lieutenant Nisbet, was with him; he tenderly got him into the boat, and laid him in the bottom of her. Nelson was bleeding profusely, and as the sight of the blood seemed to increase his faintness, Nisbet took off his hat and concealed the wounded shoulder. Next he examined the wound, which was only to be done in the flash of the artillery, and so holding the almost sundered limb as to in some measure hinder the bleeding, he bound up the wound with a silk handkerchief which he took from his neck. These particuliars are given by Clarke. The young fellow's presence of mind, Nelson afterwards declared, saved his life. It was, indeed, an act of real heroism, for the guns were thundering and the shot were flying, and the wounded were shrieking, and, above all, there was the unnerving spectacle of Nelson, bleeding to death in the bottom of the boat.

The nearest ship was the " Seahorse." The wife of the commander of that ship was on board of her. When Nelson was told that the vessel they were making for was the " Seahorse," he ordered them in a faint voice to go to another ship. Nisbet answered that delay might cost him his life. " Then I will die ! " exclaimed the noble-hearted man, " for I would rather suffer death than alarm Mrs. Fremantle by seeing me in this state and when I can give her no tidings whatever of her husband." The thought of others was always first with Nelson. One must closely study his correspondence and carefully follow his career to understand how full of compassion, benevolence, charity, this great man was. The picture off Teneriffe is deeply impressive. One sees the Atlantic surge shaping out of darkness and flashing into the ghastly light of foam ; one sees the British ships pallid, elusive as phantoms, heavily plunging amidst the hollows of those darkling waters ; but above all one sees that small boat, swept by the spray as she starts to each pulse of oar, with Nelson, the darling of our country, lying bleeding under her thwarts, speechlessly suffering agony, and, what was worse than his physical pain, irremediably maimed, so that nevermore should he know the use of a right arm.

They rowed him to his own ship, the "Theseus," one of whose midshipmen was Mr. Hoste, afterwards Sir William Hoste, among the most gallant of Collingwood's captains. The hour was two o'clock in the morning, and young Hoste stood at the gangway looking down. He heard Nelson say: "Let me alone; I have yet my legs left and one arm. Tell the surgeon to make haste and get his instruments. I know I must lose my right arm, so the sooner it is off the better." The young midshipman then saw him grasp a rope, and drag himself up the ship's side. Dwell a little upon this prodigious act of fortitude in a man whose right arm, bleeding always, hung by a shred or two, whilst the boat leapt in the hollow sea and the rolling ship leaned to and from her. The moment he gained the deck he told the surgeon to remove the limb, "and," says Hoste, "he underwent the amputation with the same firmness and courage that have always marked his character." The limb, Miss Knight afterwards discovered, was placed in the hammock of a dead seaman, and consigned to the deep with the body.

It is wonderful also to recall that, despite the weakness arising from the flow of blood, the torture of the wound and the grief attending his loss, he was writing to Sir John Jervis with his left hand on July 27, the operation having taken place in the early morning of July 25.

The attack was no inglorious defeat, but it was a bad and bloody failure. Captain Bowen and a number of lieutenants lost their lives. Twenty-eight seamen and sixteen marines were killed, a hundred and five seamen and marines were wounded, and a crowd of seamen and marines were drowned. Captain Troubridge, who was ashore, collected all the people he could find, and by daybreak his force consisted of eighty marines, eighty pikemen, and one hundred and eighty small-arms men. He found the whole of the streets commanded by field-pieces, and swarms of Spaniards and French under arms approaching by every avenue. The boats were stove, and no more men could be got. The ammunition was wet, and there were no provisions. Troubridge sent Captain Hood with a flag of truce to the Governor to say that he would burn the town if the Spanish force approached one inch further. This miserable fiasco ended in a manner not less honourable to the Spaniard than to the British. The Governor refreshed the poor fellows with wine and bread, and they returned to their ships, marching "through the town on our return with the British colours flying at our head."

It is pleasant to find Nelson writing to his wife thus on Aug. 3 : " My dearest Fanny, — I am so confident of your affection that I feel the pleasure you will receive will be equal, whether my letter is wrote by my right hand or left. It was the chance of war, and I had great reason to be thankful ; and I know that it will add much to your pleasure in finding that Josiah, under God's providence, was principally instrumental in saving my life. As to my health, it never was better ; and now I hope soon to return to you ; and my country, I trust, will not allow me any longer to linger in want of that pecuniary assistance which I have been fighting the whole war to preserve to her. But I shall not be surprised to be neglected and forgot, as probably I shall no longer be considered as useful. However, I shall feel rich if I continue to enjoy your affection. The cottage is now more necessary than ever."

Filled with despair by the loss of his arm he wrote thus to the Earl of St. Vincent from the " Theseus " : " I am become a burthen to my friends, and useless to my country ; but by my letter wrote the 24th, you will perceive my anxiety for the promotion of my son-in-law Josiah Nisbet. When I leave your command, I become dead to the World ; I go hence and am no more seen. If from poor Bowen's loss you think it proper to oblige me, I rest confident you will do it; the Boy is under obligations to me, but he repaid me by bringing me from the Mole of Santa Cruz." And this is how the gallant Jervis helped to keep lifted that noble spirit: "Mortals cannot command success; you and your companions have certainly deserved it, by the greatest degree of heroism and perseverance that ever was exhibited. I grieve for the loss of your arm, and for the fate of poor Bowen and Gibson, with the other brave men who fell so gallantly. I hope you and Captain Fremantle are doing well; the 'Seahorse' shall waft you to England the moment her wants are supplied. Your son-in-law is Captain of the 'Dolphin' Hospital ship, and all other wishes you may favour me with shall be fulfilled, as far as is consistent with what I owe to some valuable officers in the 'Ville de Paris.' We expect to hear of the Preliminaries of Peace being agreed on every hour. I have betted £100 that they were settled on or before the 12th and that the Definitive Treaty is signed before that day month. Give my love to Mrs. Fremantle. I will salute her and bow to your stump to-morrow morning, if you will give me leave."

He went home in the "Seahorse," whose commander, Fremantle, had been wounded at Teneriffe. Never possibly had he passed hours more dispiriting with visitation of anxious thought than these of this passage to England. He had lost his arm, he had lost an eye, he had been hurt in the back; in other ways had he been injured while fighting the battles of his country; he was now what he himself called a left-handed Admiral, and believed that his country would no longer need his services, and would make haste to forget him. Added to the mental dejection induced by these reflections was the pain in the stump of his arm. It tortured him day and night. Ship's surgery was but rough work in those days. There was no ether, no chloroform; and laudanum made one speechless and sick, and so, perhaps, increased the sufferings by forbidding one the relief of a howl or a groan. The ligature had been applied to one of the arteries after amputation, and produced agonising spasms. But what Nelson most complained of was the coldness of the knife in making the first circular cut through the integument and muscles. Always afterwards, whenever there was any prospect of his ship going into action, he gave orders that a hanging stove should be kept in the galley that hot water might be ready for heating the knife. It is told of him that when he was off Toulon expecting an engagement with the French, he called to the ship's surgeon and said with great significance, "Doctor, don't forget the warm water!" The doctor answered that a hanging stove was in readiness, and Nelson smiled, and gave him an approving nod.

The "Seahorse" reached Spithead on September 1, and Nelson joined his wife at Bath. Bath was in much favour in those days. It is true that Jane Austen had not yet written some of the best of her novels there, but Anstey and many others had celebrated the place in songs, and lampoons, and prose sketches. Folks believed in the virtues of the waters, sipped and simpered, bathed together, walked in Milsom Street in the afternoon, and gambled at the card-tables at night. Nelson thought the place hotter than the West Indies. The climate appears to have changed since his time. He found his wife well, and she took him in hand and nursed him with devotion. He was in London in September. While he was in lodgings, news came of Admiral Duncan's victory over the Dutch. London was in an uproar. The streets were crowded with yelling and cheering mobs. Nelson was lying in his bed in great pain, hoping to gain some rest at the cost of a draught of laudanum, when a crowd of people, observing that the house was not illuminated, began to thunder upon the door. A servant informed them that Sir Horatio Nelson, who had been badly wounded at Teneriffe, lodged there and could not be disturbed. "Nelson!" was the general exclamation, and one of the foremost of the party cried out, "You will hear no more from us to-night." "My general reception from John Bull has been just what I wished," he wrote to Lord St. Vincent.

Nature effected for Nelson what the science of that day was unequal to. Dec. 8, 1797, we meet with this touching entry, a note sent to the Rev. Mr. Greville, of St. George's, Hanover Square: —

"An officer desires to return thanks to Almighty God for his perfect recovery from a severe wound, and also for the many mercies bestowed upon him. (For next Sunday.)"

Lord Eldon relates that the King, on Nelson's appearance at Court, after acknowledging his great services, added, with significant reference to the loss of his arm: " But your country has a claim for a bit more of you." But by this time Nelson's mind was easy. He had discovered that "the country" did not mean to dispense with the services of a left-handed Admiral whose soul reposed in the skin of a Nelson. The Admiralty decided to give him the "Foudroyant," but, as she could not be got ready in time to enable him to join Lord St. Vincent without delay, he hoisted his flag on board the "Vanguard," and was off Cadiz with the fleet under Jervis on April 30.

Rumours had reached the ears of St. Vincent of a powerful congregation of shipping in Toulon, and Nelson was sent into the Mediterranean with a small squadron to learn all he could about it. The report reached this country, and universal uneasiness prevailed, from the King to the shoeblack. What was the design of that French force? Was its object the capture of Ireland? Did it mean to sweep the Channel? Were our West Indian possessions its quarry? Government reinforced Lord St. Vincent, and directed him to detach a squadron up the Mediterranean under the command of a discreet flag-officer, who, if he fell in with a French force, was to use his utmost endeavours to take, sink, or destroy it.

The choice of Nelson excited some ill-blood.

Sir William Parker and Sir John Orde were
both Nelson's seniors. Orde sent St. Vincent
a challenge, but the duel did not come off.
Indeed, in other ways at this time Orde rendered himself offensive. The Earl, when Nelson was objected to as a junior officer, justly
replied, "Those who are responsible for measures have a right to choose their men." A
letter from one of the puisne Lords of the
Admiralty, insolently denouncing St. Vincent
for sending so young a flag-officer as Nelson to
seek the French fleet, was publicly read on
board Sir William Parker's ship, the "Prince
George." That seasoned old salt, Jervis, stuck
to his opinion and his choice, and wrote thus to
Lady Hamilton : "I am bound by my oath of
chivalry to protect all who are persecuted and
distressed, and I would fly to the succour of
their Sicilian majesties was I not positively
forbid to quit my post before Cadiz. I am
happy, however, to have a knight of superior
prowess in my train who is charged with this
enterprise at the head of as gallant a band as
ever drew sword or trailed a pike." It is queer
to find the dialect of Euphues in the mouth of
an old tar who had spent a large portion of his
days in fighting his country's enemies and in
chewing his country's bad salt junk. But it

will be seen that his Lordship was addressing Lady Hamilton.

This woman's acquaintance Nelson had made when he was in the " Agamemnon " in the Mediterranean. He had called on the British Ambassador, Sir William Hamilton, at Naples, and here he had been introduced to the Sicilian King and his Court. He had also met Lady Hamilton. His earlier biographers call her "the bewitching siren." It is doubtful, however, if the fascination of purely sensuous charms can ever wholly dominate the neutral-ising element of vulgarity in a woman. It is true that Lady Hamilton played very well and sang ; she could also act, and she spoke Italian, but not good English. I think it is of Mrs. Pritchard that Dr. Johnson somewhere says that when she was on the stage she was all that was refined, and when she was off she would speak of her *gownd*. Nelson does not appear to have been immediately captured by Emma's charms. To his wife he could find no more to say about her than this : " She is a young woman of amiable manners, and who does honour to the station in which she is raised." Raised from what ? The subject is not savoury, but it can-not be shirked. She had been a nursemaid, and then she worked for a time as servant in the family of a tradesman. She lived with Sir Harry Featherstonehaugh, and afterwards with the Hon. Charles Greville. An obscene baboon called Graham hired her for his "Temple" as the "Goddess of Health." In 1786 Greville relinquished the beauty to his uncle, Sir William Hamilton, whose mistress she was till Sept. 6, 1791, on which date the old man married her. The finger of scorn has been pointed at Sir William, and certainly the figure he makes in his domestic relations but ill accords with those lofty sentiments and exalted principles which we are accustomed to think of as animating the breasts of our British Ambassadors. It must be remembered, how-ever, that he was a widower. By his licentious-ness he insulted no wife, by his marriage he affronted no children. When we hear of him in this connection we find something senile in his conduct, and pity is mingled with contempt. Mr. J. C. Jeaffreson describes Lady Hamilton, when she was about twenty-three or twenty-four years old, as lithe, lissom, agile, and slim. Waist of the right type for health and classic grace. Full breasts and swelling hips — in short, her youth betokened that there would be a great plenty of her when she grew old. And, indeed, she became very fat. Her hair was a deep brown, but Mr. Jeaffreson finds that it lacked "the feathery softness of the Byronic curls."

In 1815 a book called "The Memoirs of Lady Hamilton," was published anonymously. There is strong internal evidence for supposing that these "Memoirs" were inspired by Lady Nelson, just as Lady Hamilton dictated most of that "Life of Nelson" which is known by the name of Harrison's. The writer of these "Memoirs" gives Emma plenty of ironical praise, and this praise, couched as it is, would be relished by Lady Nelson, of whom, perhaps, some of these days, we shall be having a "Life," and I am bound to say that the justification of this good, virtuous, affectionate lady is directly invited by Captain Mahan's remarks about the Nelson family clinging to Lady Hamilton, and their coldness to Lady Nelson, not to mention that odd passage concerning an anonymous letter. The writer of these "Memoirs" describes Emma when a servant girl, thus : —

"To a figure of uncommon elegance were added features perfectly regular, with a countenance of such indescribable sweetness of expression as fixed the beholder in admiration. The airiness of her form gave a peculiar grace to her movements, and such was the flexibility of her limbs that she might have been considered as a mountain nymph. Her agility, however, though light and sportive, had nothing in it of boisterous activity ; nor in the gaiety which she supported did there appear any of that levity which seems to court, instead of repelling, temptation. Among the many attractions which at this period distinguished the female of whom we are speaking, that of a very musical voice was one which could hardly fail, in the situation where she was placed, to excite attention and inflame vanity. Having the advantage of a good ear, aided by a retentive memory, she was enabled to sing popular airs with considerable effect ; and the opportunities which she enjoyed of frequenting places of public amusement served to increase the passion for dramatic entertainment. The effect produced by these exhibitions was that of adding to her love of singing a strong turn for mimicry, which was encouraged by her companions to such a degree as to become the subject of general conversation."

Her capacity as an actress was certainly extraordinary. It is said that with a common piece of stuff she could so arrange it and clothe herself as to offer life-like and startling representations of such people as a Jewess, a Roman

matron, a Helen, Penelope, or Aspasia. The
shawl dance was said to owe its origin to her
invention. Her voice was such that she was
offered two thousand guineas to sing for the
season at the Opera House, London. Yet this
lively lady, when living with Graham, used to
be sunk in a mud bath, and exhibit nothing but
her head, with her hair elaborately dressed in
the prevailing fashion, with powder, flowers,
ropes of pearls, and feathers! She was loyal to
her mother, and she must be honoured for that.
This mother was a vulgar woman, whose name
was Mary Kidd; she became Mary Lyon by
marriage. When she was a widow she took the
name of Doggen or Dogan, which was lifted
into elegance by being pronounced and spelt
Cadogan; but though her name was high her
strain kept low. Mr. W. H. Long, the latest
editor of the "Memoirs," says of her: "The
good woman, though mixing much with high
society through her daughter, still retained some
of the plebeian tastes of her early condition. At
an entertainment given in honour of the English
fleet at Naples, at the drinking of a toast Mrs.
C. exclaimed, ' They may talk of their Lach-
rymæ Christi and stuff, but give me a glass of
London gin before a whole bottle of it!' As
there happened to be a few bottles of gin on

board one of the ships her wish was speedily
gratified. But she certainly possessed some
sterling qualities, for Lord Nelson wrote of her
with respect and sent her presents, and Sir W.
Hamilton, who must have known her intimately
during her residence under his roof, left her an
annuity of £100 for life."

Nelson himself is described by a lady who
was much in his company at Naples, as "little,
and not remarkable in his person either way;
but he has great animation of countenance and
activity in his appearance; his manners are un-
affectedly simple and modest." He was not yet
forty years of age. It is strange that the lady
(Cornelia Knight) should not have commented
upon the deep furrows in his face. The best of
his portraits show him as heavily lined, as
though with constant anxiety. Much, however,
of this may have been due to pain and to con-
stitutional delicacy.

He was now to hunt the Mediterranean for
the French fleet. It had sailed from Toulon —
a formidable armament full of soldiers and sailors — in the same weather that had wrecked the
"Vanguard" aloft. What was the destination
of this force? Nelson writes to his wife: "I
yet live in hopes of meeting these fellows; but
it would have been my delight to have Bona-

parte on a wind, for he commands the fleet as well as the army.   Glory is my object, and that alone."   Did he ever write this last sentence? The letter is printed by Clarke and McArthur, who scandalously melodramatised this great man. The hunt after the Frenchman is only to be paralleled by the hunt after the same enemy in 1805.

At last the " Culloden," commanded by Captain Troubridge, having been sent into the Gulf of Coron for intelligence, returned with a French brig she had captured, and Nelson heard that the French fleet had been seen steering to the south-east from Candia, about four weeks before. This intelligence was confirmed by a vessel that passed close to the British, and Nelson immediately made all sail for Alexandria.   In the evening the signal was flown for the fleet to close, and early on the morning of August 1 the "Zealous" made the signal of the French fleet at anchor in Aboukir Bay, — sixteen sail of the line, so she signalled.

The French force consisted of thirteen sail of the line and four frigates.   It is said that for many preceding days Nelson had scarcely eaten or slept, but when the French ships were discovered he ordered dinner to be served.   His early biographers tell us that on his officers rising from table, he exclaimed, " Before this time to-morrow I shall have gained a peerage or Westminster Abbey." A delightful sight those ships must have made for the eyes of the British to feast on, sick as the sailors were of scouring the Mediterranean in search of them. They lay in a curved line, the stately central link of which was the " Orient," a monster of one hundred and twenty guns, believed to have been manned by one thousand seamen and soldiers. With what sensations did the French view the approaching enemy ! They counted, it is true, their line of defence impregnable, flanked as it was by batteries, but they also knew that Nelson was in that approaching fleet ; and as they lay at anchor they watched with profound anxiety the steady advance of our noble ships.

Perhaps the most decisive sea-battle that was ever fought was about to begin.

CHAPTER VI

THE NILE

THE waters of Aboukir Bay on August 1, 1798, a little time before seven o'clock, at which hour Captain Berry, of the "Vanguard," tells us it fell dark, presented a picture there is no magic in ink to conjure up to the vision of another; the brush of the great marine painter could alone express it. The scarlet of the sunset was in the air when the ships of Nelson heeled to the breeze as they hauled the wind, clewing up their royals as they did so. The low land ran in purple, darkening towards Alexandria, with the loom of Pharos Tower fading in the evening air. In safety afar might be hovering some boat or other of lateen rig, a dash of keen white upon the pulsing blue of the waters. Hands swung over the side of each ship, heaving the lead. Ground tackle was got along the decks to enable the ships to anchor by the stern. All was silent upon the darkening waters as the British floated towards that long line of enemy.

There might have been irresolution *there*. Would the British attack that night? Yes! mark how they haul their wind in succession. The Admiral (De Brueys) signals for topgallant yards to be crossed : changes his mind and tells his people by flags that he will engage the enemy at anchor. He declares he has not seamen enough to fight under sail ; every ship, according to De Brueys, wanted two hundred more good men than she had. In fact, the Frenchman declares that most of the people were ashore when the " Heureux " made the signal for a sail W.N.W., and only a small number obeyed the order to repair on board their respective ships. There is always a reason for being beaten, and statistics are invariably on the side of the angels.

Whatever doubts and hesitations may have shot tremors through the souls of the gallant fellows who manned that looming line of battleships in Aboukir Bay, nothing like irresolution was to be heard of in Nelson's seventy-fours. For days and days, his biographers say, this great Admiral had meditated the matter of the French fleet, and considered the enemy in every posture imaginable to the experience of a seaman, and time after time he had called his captains aboard and conferred with them, and submitted his plans, and given his directions, insomuch, it is declared, that when the French fleet were sighted every British commander knew so exactly what was to be done as to render signals hardly necessary.

What, then, becomes of the claim of Captain Foley of the "Goliah"? This ship and the "Zealous" had the honour of leading. It is claimed for Foley that on his own responsibility he deviated from Nelson's plan and orders by passing *inside* the enemy. Sir Charles Napier stoutly contended for this. Sir Charles says: "Lord Nelson was not the man who proved the adventure; the exploit was achieved by Sir Thomas Foley." (Think of the Battle of the Nile won by Foley! Startling news, surely, for the historian.) "The chivalrous commander of the 'Goliah' began the action," proceeds Sir Charles; "he it was who in this critical moment saw that there was room to pass between the shore and the enemy's fleet." Seeing that other ships followed Foley's example, Napier's arguments would lead us to suppose that there was rebellion and mutiny amongst the officers under Nelson.

"Garth did not write his own Dispensary."

It does not seem, however, to have occurred to Napier that Nelson himself decisively settled

the question. In a letter to Lord Howe dated
January, 1799, he wrote thus : " It was only
this moment that I had the invaluable approbation of the great, the immortal Earl Howe —
an honour the most flattering a Sea officer could
receive, as it comes from the first and greatest
Sea officer the world has ever produced. I had
the happiness to command a Band of Brothers ;
therefore night was to my advantage. Each
knew his duty, and I was sure each would feel
for a French ship. By attacking the Enemy's
van and centre, the wind blowing directly along
their line, I was enabled to throw what force I
pleased on a few ships. This plan my friends
readily conceived by the signals (for which we
are principally, if not entirely, indebted to your
Lordship), and we always kept a superior force
to the Enemy. At twenty-eight minutes past
six, the sun in the horizon, the firing commenced. At five minutes past ten, when
" L'Orient " blew up, having burnt seventy
minutes, the six Van ships had surrendered. I
then pressed further towards the Rear ; and had
it pleased God that I had not been wounded
and stone blind there cannot be a doubt but
that every ship would have been in our possession. But here let it not be supposed that any
officer is to blame. No, on my honour I am

satisfied each did his very best.   I have never
before, my Lord, detailed the action to anyone,
but I should have thought it wrong to have
kept it from one who is our great Master in
Naval tactics and bravery."

We will take it, in spite of the gallant Foley
and Sir Charles Napier (they were related by
marriage), that Nelson's magnificent tactical
success was the offspring of his own brain, of
his only.   Before the guns of the contending
fleet deafen us, however, it is worth pointing
out that had the ships been steamers fitted even
with auxiliary screws (the Frenchmen prepared
for steaming), the battle could never have been
fought on the lines laid down by Nelson.   The
rearmost ships of the French would have
steamed up to the assistance of those of the
van, upon whom the British had thrown their
full weight.   Would there have been room?
They would have found room.   By very simple
evolutions they could have brought their broadsides to bear.

A grievous disaster befell the British force
on the very threshold.   The "Culloden," commanded by Captain Troubridge, went ashore.
All that seamanship could do to warp her off
was done — to no purpose.   It is not hard to
figure the sensations of the heroic Troubridge

and the wrath and dismay of his gallant ship's company. Thus was Nelson's force weakened by seventy-four guns, by the deprivation of the services of a large body of splendid sailors, and by the virtual extinction of one of the ablest and most trusted of his captains.

When the battle commenced it was as black as a thunderstorm, wild and frightful with the ceaseless flashing of guns and the rolling roar of artillery. As the English ships approached, the French poured a heavy fire into them. But the British were bow on and made no reply. Then the "Goliah" swept the "Guerrier" with a broadside and let go her stern anchors abreast of the ship. She dragged, and brought up alongside the "Conquérant." The "Zealous" brought up on the "Guerrier's" bow. Thus one by one, some inside, some outside the line of enemy, did the British ships station themselves, pouring, two ships to one, tremendous broadsides into the trapped and already beaten foe. "The French fought stubbornly, with great firmness and deliberation," says Berry. But when Nelson's tactics had been gathered, what would be the feelings of the people on board the rearmost of the Frenchmen who lay helpless and dumb at their anchors? A more wonderful and appalling scene of conflict cannot be figured. The five foremost ships of the French having been beaten, that huge vessel, the "Orient," took fire. When she was seen to be in a blaze, the crews of the war-ships in her neighbourhood cleared their decks of all combustibles, and wetted their sails, and men with buckets of water were stationed in all parts of them. But even when the French giantess was in flames throughout her lower decks, the rage of her crew held them valiantly fighting their upper guns.

A ship on fire is a terrific spectacle at any time. But here was one of the hugest ships then afloat in flames, full of gunpowder and deadly explosives, in the heart of as many vessels as would fill Tilbury Docks. The stoutest held their breath. When would the explosion happen? Fore and aft at ten o'clock the flames were licking the stooping heavens; her spritsail yard and bowsprit were black with men. By the ghastly effulgence was the whole scene of battle rendered visible. Every rope, every spar was touched, and sprang in lines of light into the painting of a mutilated war-ship. It was as though a city were on fire. As far off as Rosetta the glowing scarlet over the roaring and crackling "Orient" was as visible as a sunset. "Motionless bodies of Arabs," it has been written, "might be seen ashore watching the sight." The explosion was as of some enormous force of nature. Every ship was shaken to her heart. The air was aflame with the volcanic upheavals of burning wreckage, and the water shrieked in clouds of steam as it was pierced by the falling javelins of fire.

No lightning stroke could be more dazzling; the vision groped in vain, for when that mighty light went out a midnight darkness seemed to roll upon the sea. A universal hush followed the explosion. The water was full of drowning and swimming men, says a writer in "Black-wood's." "Oh, bon John, give rop'e — give rop'e," the miserable wretches cried. Many were picked up. To a French sailor thus rescued, an English officer said, "Well, Monsieur, what think you now of your Bonaparte?" The poor fellow, half dead, blustered out, "Oh, Monsieur John Bull, dis nothing, dis nothing. Vive Napoléon! Vive Napoléon!"

The "Orient" was the flag-ship of Admiral de Brueys. But long before the explosion occurred he had been killed. He had already been wounded in the head and arm when a cannon-ball struck him, and almost cut him in two. He begged to be left to lie upon the

deck, and soon afterwards expired. It is a pity
that glory should be so bloody. But what was
blood to Bonaparte? The blood that reddened
the waters of Aboukir Bay was shed by him,
not by the British. We were ever lovers of
peace, and when we fought it was for the preservation of our throne and country — nay, for our
very hearths.

Commodore Casabianca and his son, a boy
aged ten, were on board the "Orient." But
the lad was not blown sky-high, as Mrs.
Hemans feigns. When the ship blew up
father and son were in the water, holding by
some wreckage, seeking each other. The explosion killed them. A French account makes
out that after the explosion of the "Orient"
hostilities were suspended for a quarter of an
hour, owing to the consternation and horror
excited in both fleets by that momentary glimpse
of hell. But then the breeze was filled again
by the thunder of guns, and one realises the
storm of *morbleus*, *diables*, and *sacrés* which rose
to the heaven from the rearmost ships of the
French as the tide of battle rolled roaring down
the line.

Nelson had been wounded comparatively
early in the engagement. The "Vanguard,"
flying his flag, had anchored by the stern abreast

of the French "Spartiate." Nelson was looking over a rough sketch of the Bay of Aboukir which had been found in a French ship by Captain Hallowell, when he was hit athwart the forehead by a langridge shot; the skin fell in a flap over his eyes and blinded him. He reeled, and Berry caught him. "I am killed," he cried. "Remember me to my wife." They carried him below to the cockpit, and the surgeon was for immediately attending him, but he exclaimed: "No, I will take my turn with my brave fellows." His suffering convinced him that he was a dying man. He refused to believe the assurances of the surgeon that there was no danger, and calling the chaplain to his side, he asked him to convey his dying remembrance to Lady Nelson.

Captain Louis, commanding the "Minotaur," had so stationed himself ahead of the "Vanguard" as effectually to relieve the Admiral's ship from the furious fire of the "Aquilon." It is related in the "Naval Chronicle" that Nelson, conceiving himself to be dying, was desirous of thanking Louis for his noble behaviour. He sent for him, and the meeting between the two heroic characters is said to have been extremely affecting. Louis held his hand in silent sorrow. Nelson bade him farewell.

" And now," said he, " whatever may become of me, my mind is at peace."

He was reassured when the wound was dressed ; he was willing to agree with the doctor that it was not dangerous ; he was entreated to remain quiet, but he was anxious to write a despatch to the Admiralty.   His secretary, who was himself wounded, was so much affected by Nelson's condition that he was unable to write to his dictation.   The chaplain was then sent for, and while he was coming Nelson's impatience was so great that in some blind fashion he was trying to scrawl out with his left hand a few words interpreting the emotions which were shaking his great and gallant heart.   Here we have a picture surely not less impressive and affecting than any that preceded it, than any save one that can follow it.   Always bear in mind the rude interior of that man-of-war dimly lighted ; the thrilling crash of shot in the solid timber above ; the muffled thunder of artillery ; the shouts of men wrestling half-naked at the guns.   That central figure of this bloody fight staggers with ensanguined brow to the table, and, filled with the transports of victory, blindly essays to write.

But now the " Orient " was on fire, and Captain Berry came below to report the fact.   It is

said that Nelson went on deck and watched the
appalling sight. The resistance in the rear was
not very stubborn. Two powerful French ships,
the "Guillaume Tell" and the "Généreux,"
and two frigates, escaped. Another ship drove
ashore, and was subsequently fired by her own
people. In all, the French ships taken or de-
stroyed amounted to thirteen. Thirteen out of
seventeen! What a very small balance to
leave old Boney! But small as it was, it
was doomed to diminution yet by the later
capture of the "Guillaume Tell" and the
"Généreux."

It is impossible to convey an idea of the sensation excited in London by the news of this
victory. Nelson's failure in discovering the
enemy's fleet had excited much uneasiness and
even indignation, and Government was censured
in no measured terms for intrusting a command
of supreme importance to a young Rear-Admiral.
Then came Captain Capel with the news on
October 2, 1798, and round flashed that worth-
less weathercock, called public opinion, right
slap into the wind's eye,— a very fair wind for
Nelson,— with a shriek that must have meant
joy, as the tail of the thing swept to leeward.
Lord Spencer, First Lord of the Admiralty,
asked God to bless "my dear Sir Horatio."

Lady Spencer, hysterical with composite emotion — for had not Nelson justified her husband? — writes: "Joy, joy, joy to you, brave, gallant, immortalised Nelson! May that great God whose cause you so valiantly support protect and bless you to the end of your brilliant career! Such a race surely never was run. My heart is absolutely bursting with different sensations of joy, of gratitude, of pride, of every emotion that ever warmed the bosom of a British woman on hearing of her country's glory."

The King's Speech on November 20 ran: "By this great and brilliant victory, an enterprise of which the injustice, perfidy, and extravagance had fixed the attention of the world, and which was peculiarly directed against some of the most valuable interests of the British Empire, has in the first instance been turned to the confusion of its authors." Nelson was made Baron Nelson of the Nile and Burnham Thorpe. The House of Commons voted him a pension of two thousand a year, and the same sum to the two next heirs to the title. Special gold medals were ordered. Gifts of splendour reached him: a gold box set with diamonds from the Emperor of Russia, a "Plume of Triumph" blazing with diamonds from the Sultan of Turkey. The East India Company presented him

with ten thousand pounds. There were many
other costly gifts.

Two ships, the "Culloden" and "Alexander,"
were sent to Naples to refit. The King went
out to them in his barge, accompanied by a
boatload of fiddlers. You will suppose that
Lady Hamilton was not far off. She and Sir
William went on board in a barge of their own,
and they too were accompanied by musicians.
All is gingerbread and tinsel. The Queen of
Naples on receiving the news of the victory had
fainted, recovered, cried, laughed, danced, and
kissed everybody she could catch hold of. Lady
Hamilton also took care to faint. The Queen's
children scampered about mad with delight.
Contrast all this — those barges, those boatloads
of fiddlers — with the two grim ships in the bay,
silent but significant with their iron guns, the
Jacks looking out of the ports, the officers un-
emotionally moving about the quarter-deck. In
fact, fighting for the Italians was a service never
much relished by the British seamen. Nelson
himself seems to have abhorred the prospect of
returning to Naples. He hated all foreigners.

Nelson arrived at Naples Bay on board the
"Vanguard" on September 22. His health
was very low; he complained of his head as
being ready to split, of incessant sickness, of a

fever which he said had nearly done his business. Ill as he was, however, he appears to
have been much impressed and affected by his
reception at Naples. The bay was covered with
barges and boats and radiant with bunting and
gay apparel, the blue waters mirrored the sparkle
of gaudy uniforms, numberless bands of music
played " God Save the King," " Rule Britannia,"
and " See the Conquering Hero Comes." The
simplicity of Nelson's nature curiously appears
in a passage in the letter which he wrote to his
wife describing his reception : " Sir William and
Lady Hamilton came out to sea, attended by
numerous boats with emblems, etc. They, my
most respectable friends, had nearly been laid
up and seriously ill — first from anxiety and
then from joy. It was imprudently told Lady
Hamilton in a moment, and the effect was like
a shot. She fell, apparently dead, and is not
yet perfectly recovered from severe bruises."
Surely a very good story for the marines ! The
bruises proved that Emma was not such an
excellent actress as we are asked to believe.
Even a middling performer should be able to
fall down in an assumed faint without severely
bruising herself.

Sir William and his wife came alongside the
" Vanguard ; " Emma flew up the gangway lad-

der, and shrieking, "O God! is it possible!"
fell into Nelson's arms. A shower of tears seems
to have relieved her, and while she was blubbering, up steps the King. Grasping Nelson by
the hand, his Majesty called him his Deliverer
and Preserver.

Nelson went to the Hamiltons' house, and
Lady Hamilton nursed him. The windows
commanded a magnificent view of the bay.
When the full moon rose it seemed to float from
the crater of Mount Vesuvius. The lights of
the fishing-boats sparkled in the brilliant haze
of the night-beam. All was beauty outside and
elegance and hospitality within. Lady Hamilton's radical vulgarity is visible in her methods
of celebrating the Battle of the Nile. She even
went the length of walking about the streets
with the words "Nelson and Victory" on a
bandeau on her forehead. One hears of nothing but festivities, of bonfires and fireworks.
This is how Lady Hamilton celebrated Nelson's
birthday. The guests numbered eighteen hundred. A rostral column was erected under a
gorgeous canopy, and on it were inscribed
"Veni, Vidi, Vici." Nelson wrote to his wife
with a boy's glee: Lady Hamilton's prepara-
tions for celebrating his birthday, he says, are
enough to fill him with vanity; every ribbon,

every button has " Nelson." He tells his wife
of the songs and sonnets composed in honour
of him. He does not pause to reflect how his
representations of Lady Hamilton's devotion
might weigh with his wife. Perhaps it was her
duty to have joined him; perhaps she might
have read between the lines that she was not
wanted. Her son, Josiah Nisbet, was at Naples,
and so, doubtless, gave her all the news. That
she was sensible of being repelled seems to have
been conveyed in a letter which Nelson received
from Alexander Davison. He wrote that Lady
Nelson was in good health, " but very uneasy
and anxious, which is not to be wondered at. . . .
She bids me say that unless you return home in
a few months she will join the " Vanguard " at
Naples. Excuse a woman's tender feelings —
they are too acute to be expressed." At an
earlier period, Josiah Nisbet had lost his temper
and created a disturbance amongst the guests of
Lady Hamilton: possibly he was " flown with
wine and insolence ; " he was so offensive to
Nelson that Troubridge and another officer put
him out of the room.

Yet, though Nelson could write gleefully to
his wife of fêtes and bandeaux and buttons and
rostral columns, his secret loathing for the people he was called upon to protect he could

scarcely find words to convey. Even on the
day following Lady Hamilton's celebration of
his birthday, he was writing thus to Lord St.
Vincent: "I am very unwell, and the miserable
conduct of the Court is not likely to cool my
irritable temper. It is a country of fiddlers and
poets, w—— and scoundrels."

The passage that relates to the flight of the
King and Queen of Naples on board the "Vanguard" glows with as strong a light of romance
as any in the career of Nelson. The King's
cowardice and the miserable procrastinating policy of the Court, could result in nothing but
the evacuation of Naples. On December 20,
1798, a memorandum marked "*most secret*" was
sent to those concerned. Three barges and a
small cutter belonging to a frigate, armed with
cutlasses only, were to be at such and such a
place at half-past seven o'clock. This and a
little more was signed "Nelson." That the
royal flight was in contemplation before this
date is shown in certain entries in the "Journal"
under December 18 and 19. We hear of the
sail-makers making cots for the royal family on
board the "Vanguard," of painters painting the
ward-room and offices under the poop, and of
boats bringing off the valuable effects of the
King and Queen in the night.

All, then, was in readiness, but Lady Hamilton's finger must be in this pie, and so we get a Rosa Matilda romance out of it. According to Southey, Emma made every arrangement for the removal of the royal family. The King was as much afraid of his friends as he was of his enemies; the man in the street was attached to his Majesty's person, and as the unfortunate fellow believed himself strong enough to fight for the King, he had no idea of allowing him to run away. Next to the safety of the royal family must, of course, be the safeguarding of their precious goods. Southey tells us of Lady Hamilton, at the risk of her life, exploring a subterraneous passage leading from the palace to the seaside. Through this passage, all very darkly, breathlessly, and mysteriously, treasure, paintings, sculptures, and the like, valued at two millions and a half, were conveyed to the shore and stowed safely on board the English ships. Then, continues Southey in effect, Nelson went ashore, embarked the whole of the royal family in three barges, and carried them safely through a tremendous sea to the " Vanguard." As Nelson claims for Lady Hamilton a large share in this romantic procedure, we have a right to suppose that she had a hand in it.

Nelson's own description of these proceedings is highly interesting. I give it in a slightly
abridged letter to Lord St. Vincent, written in
December, 1798. " On the 14th, the Marquis
de Niza, with three of the Portuguese Squadron,
arrived from Leghorn, as did Captain Hope in
the ' Alcmene' from Egypt; from this time
the danger for the personal safety of their Sicilian Majesties was daily increasing, and new
treasons were found out even to the Minister of
War. The whole correspondence relative to
this important business was carried on with
the greatest address by Lady Hamilton and the
Queen, who, being constantly in the habits of
correspondence, no one could suspect. It would
have been highly imprudent in either Sir William or myself to have gone to Court, as we
knew that all our movements were watched, and
even an idea by the Jacobins of arresting our
persons as a hostage (as they foolishly imagined)
against the attack of Naples should the French
get possession of it.

" Lady Hamilton, from this time to the 21st,
every night received the jewels of the Royal
Family, etc., etc., and such clothes as might be
necessary for the very large party to embark, to
the amount, I am confident, of full two millions
five hundred thousand pounds sterling. On

the 18th, General Mack wrote that he had no prospect of stopping the progress of the French, and entreated their Majesties to think of retiring from Naples with their august Family as expeditiously as possible. All the Neapolitan Navy were now taken out of the Mole, consisting of three Sail of the Line and three frigates; the seamen from the two Sail of the Line in the Bay left their ships and went on shore. A party of English seamen with Officers were sent from the 'Vanguard' to assist in navigating them to a place of safety. From the 18th various plans were formed for the removal of the Royal Family from the palace to the water-side; on the 19th I received a note from General Acton, saying that the King approved of my plan for their embarkation. This day, the 20th and 21st, very large assemblies of people were in commotion, and several people were killed, and one dragged by the legs to the palace. The mob, by the 20th, were very unruly, and insisted the Royal Family should not leave Naples; however, they were pacified by the King and Queen speaking to them.

" On the 21st, at half-past eight P. M., three barges, with myself and Captain Hope, landed at a corner of the Arsenal. I went into the palace and brought out the whole Royal Family, put them into the Boats, and at half-past nine they were all safely on board the ' Vanguard,' when I gave immediate notice to all British Merchants that their persons would be received on board every and any ship in the Squadron, their effects of value being before embarked in the three English transports, who were partly unloaded, and I had directed that all the condemned provisions should be thrown overboard in order to make room for their effects. Sir William Hamilton had also directed two vessels to be hired for the accommodation of the French emigrants, and provisions were supplied from our Victuallers ; in short, everything had been done for the comfort of all persons embarked.

"On the 23rd, at 7 P. M., the ' Vanguard,' ' Sannite,' and ' Archimedes,' with about twenty sail of vessels, left the Bay of Naples ; the next day it blew harder than I ever experienced since I have been at sea. Your Lordship will believe that my anxiety was not lessened by the great charge that was with me, but not a word of uneasiness escaped the lips of any of the Royal Family. On the 25th, at 9 A. M., Prince Albert, their Majesties' youngest child, having eat a hearty breakfast, was taken ill, and at 7 P. M., died in the arms of Lady Hamilton ; and here it is my duty to tell your Lordship the obligations which the whole Royal Family, as well as myself, are under on this trying occasion, to her Ladyship. They necessarily came on board without a bed, nor could the least preparation be made for their reception. Lady Hamilton provided her own beds, linen, etc., and became *their slave*, for except one man, no person belonging to Royalty assisted the Royal Family, nor did her Ladyship enter a bed the whole time they were on board. Good Sir William also made every sacrifice for the comfort of the august Family embarked with him. I must not omit to state the kindness of Captain Hardy, and every officer in the 'Vanguard,' all of whom readily gave their beds for the convenience of the numerous persons attending the Royal Family."

The flight was attended with several circumstances of misery. First and foremost, the weather was extremely heavy, and the Italians are not good sailors. On board, at the start, everything was confusion and wretchedness. If the old line-of-battle ship knew how to fight, she also knew how to roll in a sea-way. Everything movable flew from side to side. The crash of crockery, the groans of the foreign stomach, the greasy appeal of despair to the Virgin Mary and the Saints, combined in a ghastly

music of the deep. There was no fiddling.
The bandeau was not thought of. No man sat
down to write a sonnet to Nelson. At half-past
one in the morning a blast of hurricane force
blew the " Vanguard's " close-reefed topsail out
of the bolt-ropes. The ship resounded with
shrieks, in which the royal throats joined. Indeed, the King and Queen were now persuaded
that they had only escaped the bayonet on shore
to perish by drowning. Distinction of persons
was lost. Everybody who could find room in
Nelson's cabin squeezed there. Nelson himself
was seasick, and here was a difficulty with which
his instincts as a tactician were unable to cope.
Sir William Hamilton was sought by his wife,
who found him sitting in their cabin with a
loaded pistol in each hand. In response to
Emma's hysterical shriek of alarm, he told her
in a cold voice and with a long face that he was
resolved not to die with a " guggle — guggle —
guggle " of the salt water in his throat, and
therefore he was prepared as soon as he felt the
ship sinking, to shoot himself. This is on the
authority of the late Admiral W. H. Smyth,
one of the ablest of our naval surveyors, and
author of " The Sailor's Word-Book."

But the general misery had not yet reached
its height. On the evening of the twenty-fifth

poor little Prince Albert, who had been taken
ill in the morning, died in Lady Hamilton's
arms. Here was a stroke which must make
every one forget contempt and disgust, and
think with pity and sympathy of the unfortunate King and Queen. Palermo was reached
in safety. The Queen remained for a little
time in the ship; Ferdinand, on the other
hand, whose tastes and sensibilities were those
of an Irish squireen, after making a hearty
breakfast, went ashore, and Nelson saw that
all proper honour was paid him by flying the
royal standard, and so forth. One thinks with
concern of Nelson at this time; he is without
sincerity in his professions of loyalty to the
Court of Naples; he hates them all round, but
he is now under the Hamilton spell; he cannot
break away from the fascination of those enchant-
ing eyes and that full form, and as Lord Keith
afterwards discovered — but it was a conclusion
that Troubridge and Ball had already arrived at
— the conqueror of the Nile was much too enthusiastic in the interpretation of his instructions
with regard to the Court of Naples, much too
willing to employ the British ships in the service of the Queen. Some sense of littleness of
character may have visited him, and helped his
illness to keep him irritable. His was strictly a

high conscience, and in his heart he was not the man to pretend to reconcile his devotion to the Neapolitan Court with either his duty to his country or his duty to his wife.

Much petulance is visible in his correspondence at this period. He was greatly irritated, moreover, by the appointment of Captain Sir Sydney Smith in "Le Tigre," of eighty guns, in the Levant. "*I do feel, for I am a man,*" he breaks out in italics to Lord St. Vincent, "that it is impossible for me to serve in these seas with a squadron under a junior officer. Could I have thought it!—and from Earl Spencer!" He frequently writes for permission to retire. He wants to go home. But Sir William and Lady Hamilton must accompany him. He tells Lady Parker in February, 1799, that she who remembers him always laughing would not credit the change in his appearance. He scarcely ever writes a letter, not strictly official, in which some reference or other to his "dear friends," his "invaluable friends," Sir William and Lady Hamilton, is not to be found. But what could have been his secret judgment of Sir William? Did he flatter himself that the old man had not taken a very correct observation of what was passing under his nose? What opinion would Nelson form of the principles and character of a man who could look on in silence while his hospitality and confidence were being abused? All this Neapolitan business in Nelson's life makes melancholy and sickening reading. The page is haunted by a faint, insufferable odour — decayed perfume — nauseating aromas, such as the ghost of a courtesan might waft to your physical nostril from an immaterial handkerchief in her misty grasp. Music as mournful as the wailing of madness, and as dim as the voice of one encaverned, murmurs from the pages as you read, and lo! a vision of ghastly Court fiddlers doing honour to Nelson with quivering elbows rises before you; and Nelson, with Lady Hamilton by his side, seems to like it; but he does n't. He has no ear for music. Let the thunders of the Nile reverberate afresh and overwhelm that degrading noise of fiddling, and let the white powder-smoke roll over the printed page and breathe to us the true incense.

CHAPTER VII

SKETCHES AND INCIDENTS

ON the morning of the 29th of June, 1799, eighteen ships of the line were anchored in order of battle in Naples Bay. At the mizzen-royal masthead of the "Foudroyant" the flag of Rear-Admiral Nelson was shaking. On the quarter-deck of this same ship were seated Nelson and Lady Hamilton. What did the Jacks think? Why, of course they envied him. Moreover, Lady Hamilton had contrived to render herself very popular with the seamen under Nelson. On more than one occasion had she been the instrument of rescuing a man from the lash.

Presently a Neapolitan boat was observed to be making for the ship. In her was no less a personage than Caracciolo, a man so intimately identified with Nelson's name that people who have nothing to say about the Nile and Copenhagen will talk to you with knowledge of the hanging of this poor devil. He was a prince, a man of ancient descent, originally Greek. He had risen to the post of commodore in the Neapolitan navy. He had attended the King and Queen to Palermo, then got leave to return to Naples, where he entered the service of the Parthenopeian Republic, served as an admiral, and commanded a force against some of the royal frigates. He had retired to a fort from which he had made his escape up country.

A traitor he was certainly, and therefore a villain. On the previous 29th of May Captain Foote wrote to Lord Nelson: "Caracciolo threatens a second attack with a considerable addition of force." Spite of his disguise, he was recognised and seized by some banditti, and brought away from the Calabrian cave in which he had been hiding. He was dragged on board the ship and placed in charge of an officer, who described him as a short, thick-set man of apparent strength, but haggard with misery and want: "His clothing in wretched condition, but his countenance denoting stern resolution to endure that misery like a man."

Count Thurn was commodore and commander of his Sicilian Majesty's frigate the "Minerva." On Caracciolo coming on board, the Count was ordered to assemble five of the senior officers under his command to inquire into the accusation of rebellion made against the prisoner, who was further charged with firing at the Sicilian colours hoisted on the " Minerva." This court-martial was held on board the " Foudroyant," and it has generally been felt that, seeing that the " Minerva " was within convenient reach of a boat, a British man-of-war was not a proper place in which to have tried Caracciolo. His defence, as reported by one who was present, ran as follows: " I am accused," he said, " of deserting my King in distress and leaguing with his enemies. The accusation is so far false that the King deserted me and all his faithful subjects. It is well known to you, gentlemen, that our frontier was covered by an army under General Mack superior to the advancing enemy, and you are aware that money is the sinews of war. The King collected everything that could be converted into specie on pretence of paying that army, embarked it in his Britannic Majesty's ship 'Vanguard,' even to the enormous amount of five hundred casks, and fled with it to Palermo, there to riot in luxurious safety. Who was then the traitor — the King or myself? "

All this was much to the point. The court, however, without losing time, found him guilty, and Nelson signed a certain mandate to Count Thurn in which occurs this very grim passage:

"You are hereby required and directed to cause the said sentence of death to be carried into execution upon the said Francisco Caracciolo accordingly by hanging him at the fore-yardarm of his Sicilian Majesty's frigate, 'La Minerva,' under your command, at five o'clock this evening, and to cause him to hang there until sunset, when you will have his body cut down and thrown into the sea."

This gave the unhappy man two hours in which to make his peace with God. The execution was by many deemed little less than murder, and it was widely believed that the abrupt hanging at the yard-arm of a ship of a man occupying Caracciolo's social position was wholly due to Lady Hamilton, for certainly mercifulness and not cruelty was one of Nelson's predominating qualities. It never will be known whether or not the wretched woman bore any part in this unfortunate business. The man was hanged. Did you ever see a man hanged at a yard-arm? I saw a man hanged at the yard-arm of a gun-boat in the Bay of Pechili. I well remember the explosion of a single gun from the frigate's side, the exhibition of a black flag at the royal mast-head, and simultaneously the swaying of a figure at the gun-boat's yard-arm. What a ghastly pendulum! How thankful I

was when those dreadful vibrations ceased, and
when the thing hung over the water motionless,
suggestive, at all events, of freedom from suffering! Hanging is the most undignified death a
man can die, even when he is locked up from
the public gaze and there is nobody but sheriffs,
warders, and reporters to stare at him. But to
be "tucked up" at the yard-arm in the full gaze
of the whole fleet, and within sight of a popu-
lous shore! The seamen crowded into the rigging of the ships to view the sight. It was
only an Italian Prince, they said, and an Admiral
of Naples that was hanging — a person of very
light estimation compared to the lowest man in
a British vessel! [1]

An extraordinary incident in connection with
this execution is related by Parsons. Whilst
the "Foudroyant" was in the bay the King
went on board of her; with him were his Prime
Minister, Sir John Acton, and some foreign
ambassadors. Nelson abandoned his cabin to
the King, and slept in the first lieutenant's. A
crowd of cooks accompanied the King, and Parsons declares that never did the midshipmen
fare so sumptuously as during the King's long
stay on board the ship. Some days after the
execution of Caracciolo, Parsons was roused with

[1] Parsons.

the information that the King was on deck. He does not explain the duty that obliged him to attend the King. He cursed him for his bad taste in rising so early, and hurrying up found his Majesty gazing through a spy-glass at some object in the water. Suddenly the King turned pale and let the glass fall to the deck with an exclamation of horror. On the port quarter of the ship, easily visible to a man with good sight, floated the body of Caracciolo : his face was distorted by strangulation, his eyes were starting from their sockets, the skin of his face was whitened into a look of putrefaction by the action of the brine. The easy superstition of the Italian leaped in terror at that tremendous picture on the port quarter. A number of priests were on board, and they were sent for. What could they tell the King to soothe his perturbed spirit? One of them suggested that the soul of the hanged man could not rest without his Majesty's forgiveness, and this the body had risen to implore. Nelson, coming on deck, put an end to the joke by ordering a boat to tow the corpse on shore. Whether true or not, this story, as related by Brenton, Parsons, and others, most certainly lingers as a tradition.

Nelson was immensely gratified by the capture of the two great line-of-battle ships which

had escaped at the Battle of the Nile. He was
on board the " Foudroyant" when the " Généreux" was taken. A lively account is given by
Parsons of the chase of this French seventy-
four. The deck is hailed from aloft, and a
man-of-war reported. She is a line-of-battle
ship going large on the starboard tack; that
is, with the weather clew of her mainsail hauled
up. " Clearly an enemy, Mr. Staines," says
Nelson. " Pray God it may be ' Le Généreux.'
Make a signal for a general chase, Sir Ed'ard."
This is addressed to Captain Sir Edward Berry.
The " Northumberland," which was in company, was taking the lead, and Nelson began to
fume. " This won't do, Sir Ed'ard. She is
certainly the ' Généreux,' and must surrender
only to my flag-ship. Sir Ed'ard, we must beat
the ' Northumberland.' " On which Captain
Berry gives the following orders : " Get the en-
gine to work on the sails — hang butts of water
to the stays — pipe the hammocks down, and
each man place shot in them — slack the stays,
knock up the wedges, and give the masts play
— start off the water, Mr. James, and pump the
ship." Nelson finds the vessel slightly off her
course, and rounds furiously upon the quartermaster at the wheel. " I 'll knock you off your
perch, you rascal, if you are so inattentive ! Sir

Ed'ard, send your best quartermaster to the weather-wheel." Then from on high floats down the voice of a seaman on the look-out: "A strange sail ahead of the chase." "Aloft with you, youngster," cried Nelson. "What! Going without your glass, and be d — d to you! Let me know what she is immediately." The signal midshipman in the cross-trees bawls down, "A sloop of war, or frigate, my Lord." She proves to be the "Success," with the gallant Captain Peard in command. "Signal to cut off the flying enemy," cries Nelson. "Great odds, Sir — thirty-two small guns to eighty large ones." Nevertheless, the plucky little frigate heaves to athwart the hawse of the running giantess, and slaps his port broadside into her. Then the Frenchman hoists his tricolour with the Rear-Admiral's flag. With incredible nimbleness the "Success" wears, and doses the enemy with her starboard guns. But now it is the Frenchman's turn. As she passes the "Success" she blazes her tremendous batteries into the little ship, and all expect when the smoke clears away to find nothing left of the frigate but a few blackened timbers. Instead of which out of the white cloud grows the gallant craft, crippled, but with the resolution of the bull-dog, in full pursuit of her gigantic opponent. "Signal for the 'Success' to discontinue the action and come under my stern," says Nelson. "She has done well for her size. Try a shot from the lower deck at her, Sir Ed'ard." The shot flies over her. "Beat to quarters, and fire coolly and deliberately at her masts and yards." Just then a ball from the enemy pierced the mizzen-staysail. Nelson, patting a little midshipman on the head, asks him with a smile how he likes that music? The boy is pale and frightened. Nelson, noticing this, exclaims: "D'ye know that Charles XII. ran away from the first shot he heard, though he was afterwards called 'The Great' because of his bravery? I therefore hope much from you in future." Shortly after this the Frenchman hauled down his colours.

Dramatic glimpses of this sort give us a clearer conception of the man than the most laboured periods of the insipid naval writer. We do not choose to think of Nelson always as nothing but a figure in a cocked hat and one arm, who shouts: "Glorious Victory or Westminster Abbey!" and who paces the quarter-deck amid the thunder of guns, the yells of men, and the enveloping shrouds of powder-smoke. One wants to know the inner life of the man, what he ate and drank, how he was lodged on board ship, what sort of talker he was, what sort of host.   Miss Knight admits us to a peep while Nelson was still in the " Foudroyant."   His cabin was decorated with a piece of timber carved into grotesque resemblance of an immense three-coloured plume of feathers. This had been a portion of the figurehead of the " Guillaume Tell."   The cabin wall was graced by four muskets which had been taken from the " San Josef " in the battle of St. Vincent.   Likewise in this cabin, as an ornament and a trophy, was the flagstaff of the " Orient."   It does not seem that Nelson found these unwieldy memorials inconvenient in a small cabin.   For some time his living-room had been enriched by a coffin presented to him by Captain Hallowell, who had caused the ghastly gift to be fashioned out of a part of one of the "Orient's " masts. He was very proud of this coffin.   It was placed upright, with the lid against the cabin bulkhead, in the wake of his chair which he used at dinner; and one day, observing some officers staring at it, he exclaimed : " You may look at it, gentlemen, as long as you please ; but depend upon it, none of you shall have it."   Tom Allen, his servant, ultimately persuaded him to allow the unpleasant object to be taken and left to lie below.   The remains of Nelson repose in that coffin under the dome of St. Paul's.

He kept a hospitable table.   There was plenty without ostentation.   His appetite at this time (1799) was small.   Often the wing of a fowl and a glass or two of champagne sufficed him.   His smile was sudden and sweet, but the habitual cast of his countenance was one of anxiety that was not wanting in a character of moodiness. His health was very poor; the wound he had received in the head had developed or accentuated a latent quality of irritability, and we need not doubt that his conscience was harassed by thoughts of his wife, and by his relations with Lady Hamilton.   But he had a very loving and bountiful heart.   He wrote in July to his wife to request that two thousand pounds of the money voted to him by the East India Company should be divided among his father, his brother-in-law, and two brothers.   " And," he adds, " if you think my sister Matcham would be gratified by it, do the same for her.   If I were rich I would do more, but it will very soon be known how poor I am."   And in August he tells his father that the King of Naples having made him a Duke by the title of Bronté, to which is attached a feud of about three thousand a year, the money should first go to him, and in succession to his elder brother, and so on.   " For your natural life," he continues, " the estate shall be taxed with five hundred a year." If Nelson was not a good husband, he was assuredly a devoted son and a loyal brother.

The Italians continued to buffoon it and befiddle it in honour of the hero of the Nile. In August he wrote to his wife with boyish delight about one of these gingerbread celebrations. First of all the King of Naples dined with him, and when his Majesty lifted his glass to drink to the hero of the day, by preconcerted signal a royal salute of twenty-one guns was fired from the Sicilian ships of war and from the castles. When the evening descended the Bay of Naples was covered with festive lights, and music swept like the breath of flowers in gushes of fragrance upon the fitful wind over the placid waters. An example of the representations was a large vessel fitted out like a Roman galley. Lamps were fixed to its oars, in the centre stood a rostral column with the name of Nelson upon it, and at the stern were two angels holding a picture of Nelson. He declares to his wife that "the beauty of the whole is beyond my powers of description." The vessel was covered with upwards of two thousand variegated lamps. She carried a number of musicians and singers who sang a composition of which the burden was, "But Nelson came, the invincible Nelson, and they were preserved and again made happy." This, together with the friendship of the King and Queen, the blandishments of Lady Hamilton, not to mention the sense of his own achievements, was quite enough to capsize the moral equilibrium of a less vain man than Nelson.

This year he resigned his command to Troubridge, and returned to Palermo. The Queen was proceeding to Vienna, and Nelson accompanied her on his way home. But before they left an insurrection broke out. The French army was about seventy miles distant, and the populace sought to detain the King and Queen and to induce Nelson to lead them against the detested enemy. The Queen was no Boadicea. She sneaked out of her palace, and got on board the "Alexander," to which ship Nelson had transferred his flag from the "Foudroyant." It was Nelson's purpose to convey the Queen to Trieste; she travelled in state to Florence and Ancona, and next day Nelson, Sir William and Lady Hamilton, and Miss Knight followed her. They had embarked on a very perilous journey. Their road carried them close to the advanced posts of the French. Miss Knight declares that Nelson disliked this expedition, and undertook it against his own convictions that he might keep his promise to the Queen.   Sir William Hamilton was extremely ill, and was convinced he should die by the way.   At Castel San Giovanni the coach in which Nelson and his friends were seated was upset, and the Hamiltons were hurt, but not seriously.   The wheel was mended, but broke down again.

It was a true sailor's journey.   The French army was behind them, and they got news of its rapid approach.   Ancona was finally reached, where they found a Russian squadron about to sail to Corfu.   An Austrian frigate named the "Bellona" had been fitted up for the Queen with silk hangings, carpets, and eighty beds.   But she learnt that there had been a mutiny on board the "Bellona," and she chose to sail with the Russians.   It was a lucky choice, for they afterwards learnt that the imperial frigate had been captured by eight vessels armed for this purpose by the French.   The Nelson party suffered miserably on board the Russian Commodore's ship.   The Commodore, who was a Dalmatian, lay ill in his cot, and his first lieutenant, a Neapolitan, was not only insolent as a man but ignorant as a seaman.   Nelson declared that a gale of wind would have sunk the ship.   At every place they arrived at crowds assembled to view the hero of the Nile.   Vienna was filled with signboards bearing his name, and the dress-makers gave his name to their latest fashions. It is interesting to learn that Nelson in this journey met and conversed with the great musician Haydn.   At the table of Prince Esterhazy he and the other guests were waited upon by a hundred Grenadiers, most of them over six feet. Count Batthyany regaled him with an aquatic fête on the Danube, and he witnessed experiments with vessels built to resist the torrents of the river.[1] At Prague the hotel at which Nelson stopped was splendidly illuminated, and when the proprietor sent in the bill it was found that he had charged for every candle.   At Hamburg Nelson lost a large diamond out of his sword. The merchants desired to replace it at a cost of eight hundred pounds, but the offer was declined.   Here he met Klopstock, whom Coleridge termed, when somebody exclaimed that he was like Milton, "A German Milton."   Here, too, Nelson met General Dumouriez.   They took a liking to one another, and Nelson saw much of the General while at Hamburg.   Dumouriez at that time supported himself by his writings, and Nelson forced him to accept a hundred pounds, saying: "You 've used your sword too well to live only by your pen."

[1] J. C. Jeaffreson.

A curious story is told by Southey in relation to Nelson's visit to Klopstock. While the Admiral was with the German Milton, a grave-looking man, dressed as though for officiating in the pulpit, was shown in. He carried a Bible in his hand, and viewing Lord Nelson earnestly, said that he had travelled forty miles with a Bible of his parish church to request that Nelson would write his name on the first leaf of it. Of course Nelson complied, and the parson blessed him and withdrew.

Mrs. Trench when Mrs. St. George, a most lovely, refined, and sweet woman by her portrait, met the Nelson party in Germany towards the close of the year 1799 and gives certain racy descriptions of Lady Hamilton which are scarcely short of libellous. The following extracts will present some idea of the diarist's kindness : —

"October 3. — Dined at Mr. Elliot's with only the Nelson party. It is plain that Lord Nelson thinks of nothing but Lady Hamilton who is totally occupied by the same object. She is bold, forward, coarse, assuming and vain. Her figure is colossal, but excepting her feet, which are hideous, well shaped. Her bones are large, and she is exceedingly *embonpoint*. She resembles the bust of Ariadne; the shape of all her features is fine, as is the form of her head,

and particularly her ears; her teeth are a little
irregular, but tolerably white : her eyes light
blue, with a brown spot in one, which, though
a defect, takes nothing away from her beauty and
expression : her eyebrows and hair are dark,
and her complexion coarse : her expression is
strongly marked, variable and interesting; her
movements in common life, ungraceful ; her
voice loud, yet not disagreeable.   Lord Nelson
is a little man, without any dignity.   Sir William is old, infirm, all admiration of his wife,
and never spoke to-day but to applaud her.
Miss Cornelia Knight seems the decided flat-
terer of the two, and never opens her mouth
but to show forth their praise ; and Mrs. Cadogan, Lady Hamilton's mother, is what one
might expect.   After dinner we had several
songs in honour of Lord Nelson, written by
Miss Knight, and sung by Lady Hamilton.
She puffs the incense full in his face; but he
receives it with pleasure, and snuffs it up very
cordially.   The songs all ended in the sailor's
way with ' Hip, hip, hip, hurrah !' — and a bumper with the last drop on the nail, a ceremony I
had never heard of or seen before.

  " October 5. — Went by Lady Hamilton's invitation to see Lord Nelson dressed for court.
On his hat he wore the large diamond feather,

or ensign of sovereignty given him by the Grand
Signior; on his breast the Order of the Bath,
the Order he received as Duke of Bronté, the
diamond star, including the sun or crescent
given him by the Grand Signior, three gold
medals obtained by three different victories, and
a beautiful present, richly set and surrounded
with laurels, which spring from two united anchors at bottom, and support the Neapolitan
crown at top; on the other is the Queen's
cypher, which turns so as to appear within the
same laurel, and is formed of diamonds on green
enamel.   In short, Lord Nelson was a perfect
constellation of stars and orders.

"October 7. — Breakfasted with Lady Hamilton, and saw her represent in succession the
best statues and paintings extant.   She assumes
their attitude, expression, and drapery with great
facility, swiftness, and accuracy.   It is remarkable that though coarse and ungraceful in common life, she becomes highly graceful, and even
beautiful, during this performance.   It is also
singular that, in spite of the accuracy of her
imitation of the finest ancient draperies, her
usual dress is tasteless, vulgar, loaded, and un-
becoming.   She has borrowed several of my
gowns, and much admired my dress, which cannot flatter, as her own is so frightful.   Her waist

is absolutely between her shoulders.   After
showing her attitudes, she sung, and I accompanied.   Her voice is good, and very strong,
but she is frequently out of tune: her expression
strongly marked and various ; and she has no
shake, no flexibility, and no sweetness. She acts
her songs, which I think the last degree of bad
taste.

"October 9.—A great breakfast at the Elliot's
given to the Nelson party. All the company, except their party and myself, went away before dinner ; after which Lady Hamilton, who declared
she was passionately fond of champagne, took
such a portion of it as astonished me.   Lord
Nelson was not behindhand, called more vocif-
erously than usual for songs in his own praise,
and after many bumpers proposed the Queen of
Naples, adding, 'She is my queen; she is queen
to the backbone.'   Sir William also this evening performed feats of activity, hopping round
the room on his backbone, his arms, legs, stars,
and ribbon all flying about in the air."

The Nelson party sailed on October 31st, in
the "King George" mail packet, and landed at
Great Yarmouth on November 6.   Those were
the ambling days of the sea.   A week from
Hamburg to Great Yarmouth !   But indeed
the voyage might have been protracted indefi-

nitely, for the vessel had barely crossed the bar when it came on to blow an off-shore gale which otherwise would have sent her scudding away to sea with the velocity of a floating balloon. As it was the weather was so heavy that nothing but the resolved spirit of Nelson could have induced the pilot to make the attempt to land. A strong glass of grog helped him to see things from Nelson's point of view, and they all somehow got ashore. A carriage was in waiting on the beach. The horses were taken from it, and a crowd, cheering at the top of their voices, dragged Nelson and his friends to the Wrestlers' Inn. The harbour was gay with flags. " The Conquering Hero " was played by bands of music, and troops paraded before the inn. He marched in solemn procession with the corporation to church to thank God for his preservation and his restoration to his country. Many have wondered that Lady Nelson did not meet him. But of course she knew he was with the Hamiltons. If Nelson could feel as a man, his wife, too, must be allowed to feel as a woman. Yet I confess the situation is one extremely hard to explain. Down to this hour he was speaking of his wife affectionately. Whilst he was at Leghorn he expressed the hope that Lady Nelson and himself would be much with Sir William and

Lady Hamilton, and that they would all very often dine together, and that when the Hamiltons went to their musical parties he and Lady Nelson would go to bed. At Hamburg just before sailing for England he purchased a magnificent lace trimming for a Court dress for Lady Nelson, and a black lace cloak for another lady, who he said had been very attentive to his wife during his absence. It is also remembered that after Aboukir some one said to him that doubtless the 1st of August was the happiest day of his life. He answered, "No." The happiest day of his life was the day on which he married his wife.

The party went to London, and on their arrival in town, Sir William and Lady Hamilton went with Nelson to dine with his father and Lady Nelson. What reception did the Reverend Edmund vouchsafe the divine Emma? A better reception, depend upon it, than Nelson got at the hands of his sovereign. Collingwood, writing under date Jan. 25, 1801, says: "Lord Nelson is here. . . . He gave me an account of his reception at Court which was not very flattering after having been the adoration of that of Naples. His Majesty merely asked him if he had recovered his health, and then, without waiting for an answer, turned to General ——

and talked to him near half an hour in great good humour. It could not be about his 'successes.'" In this manner was the hero of the Nile received by King George III. Yet it must be said that that old King, whether crazy or not, was a great stickler for the proprieties. He objected to the King of Denmark giving a masked ball when in this country, and never himself countenanced that diversion, popular as it was, because he considered it a vicious form of entertainment. Such a man would make haste to find something very objectionable in the Hamilton scandal. But then the respectable old gentleman should not have forgotten that in receiving Nelson he was in the presence of the greatest hero in British history, a man who was making his sovereign's reign more illustrious than any in the annals, not excepting Elizabeth's.

Now that Lady Hamilton was in town the life led by Nelson and his wife grew insupportable to both. They lived together very unhappily for about two months, and then happened what the ladies call a "scene." It may be read in Nicolas and a dozen lives of Nelson. They were at breakfast at their lodgings in Arlington Street when, in the course of conversation, Nelson referred to something which had been said

or done by "dear Lady Hamilton." Lady
Nelson started up and exclaimed with some
heat — "I am sick of hearing of *dear* Lady
Hamilton, and am resolved that you shall give
up either her or me." Nelson answered : "Take
care, Fanny, what you say. I love you sincerely, but I cannot forget my obligations to
Lady Hamilton, or speak of her otherwise than
with affectionate admiration." Lady Nelson said
that her mind was made up, left the room, and
shortly after drove from the house. It ended
in a separation.

Miss Knight, in referring to this period, says :
"I dined one day with Sir William and Lady
Hamilton in Grosvenor Square. Lord and
Lady Nelson were of the party, and the Duke
of Sussex and Lady Augusta Murray came in
the evening. Lord Nelson was to make his
appearance at the theatre next day, but I declined to go with the party. I afterwards heard
that Lady Nelson fainted in the box. . . . So
much was said about the attachment of Lord
Nelson to Lady Hamilton that it made the
matter still worse. He felt irritated, and took
it up in an unfortunate manner by devoting
himself more to her, for the purpose of what
he called supporting her." Miss Knight tells
us that she was obliged to cut the party. The

idea of this poor sycophantic old maid *cutting Nelson* is one to muse upon.

It is strange to observe how the unfortunate Emma mingles herself with the life of Nelson. The student cannot get away from her. She is as a strand in the rope of his career, and makes herself as much a portion of his later life as if she had been a ship or a battle.

CHAPTER VIII

THE BALTIC

ON January 1, 1801, in a general promotion of Admirals, Lord Nelson was made Vice-Admiral of the Blue, and some days later hoisted his flag in the "San Josef" at Plymouth, his favourite Hardy being his captain. He took his final leave of Lady Nelson on the 13th, and on quitting her exclaimed: "I call God to witness, there is nothing in you or your conduct I wish otherwise." The last letter he ever wrote to her is dated at Southampton on the day of his departure from London: "My dear Fanny, —We are arrived, and heartily tired; and with kindest regards to my father and all the family, believe me, your affectionate NELSON."

In consequence of the Northern Coalition, the British Government resolved to send a powerful fleet into the Baltic under Admiral Sir Hyde Parker,[1] with Lord Nelson as second in command. The Northern Coalition signified a

---

[1] Hyde Parker's name survives in Lieutenant Archer's account of a storm in which Parker showed great spirit.

treaty by which Russia, Sweden, and Denmark bound themselves to resist the right claimed by the enemy of searching their merchant vessels. Trouble had arisen in the previous July. A British squadron had fallen in with a Danish forty-gun frigate convoying two ships. The Dane was hailed by the senior British officer, who said that he should send his boat on board the convoy to search the ships for contraband of war. An action followed, and the Danish frigate and her convoy were brought into the Downs. Lord Whitworth was at once despatched to the Court of Denmark to adjust, if he could, the very grave difficulty which had arisen. Russia professed to resent the attack upon the Danish frigate, and to take offence at the passage through the Sound of the ships that had accompanied Lord Whitworth. The Emperor of Russia was Paul the Brutal — a madman. His first act was to sequester all British property in his dominions; then, made raving by news of the capture of Malta and the hoisting of the English flag alone upon it, he laid an embargo on all the British shipping in his ports, and, says Brenton, some two thousand seamen were marched away in the dead of winter to different villages and towns in the interior. The armed neutrality between Russia and Sweden was then strengthened by the junction of Denmark, and the issue of this confederation was the Battle of Copenhagen.

Nelson arrived at Spithead on the 21st of February, and on the 26th embarked six hundred troops under Colonel Stewart. Immediately the Colonel arrived Nelson sent for him. He said, "Not a moment is to be lost in embarking the troops, as I intend to sail next tide." All the soldiers were on board before midday. No man better knew the value of time. Once, in conversing with General Twiss, Nelson said, "Time, Twiss, time — time is everything; five minutes makes the difference between a victory and a defeat." On the 2d of March he sailed in the "St. George" from Portsmouth, with seven sail of the line, frigates, and small vessels, to join Sir Hyde Parker's squadron at Yarmouth. When the "St. George" was off Dungeness the wind scanted, and it was necessary to 'bout ship. Nelson himself gave the orders, and the ship missed stays, — that is to say, instead of coming round on the other tack, she remained flat aback, — "in irons," as Jack calls it. It will not be supposed that Nelson much relished his own imagination of what his men would think of this stroke of seamanship. Obviously, however, in proportion as the wind is light, so is it difficult to tack.   You keep your ship "full for stays," and then, when your helm is down, the rushing vessel sweeps with the velocity of knots into the wind's eye, and it is "let go and haul" very swiftly and very certainly.   But a ship moving sluggishly through the water responds sulkily to her helm.   In those days vessels had not very much more length than they had breadth, and how they were worked against a head wind and head sea except by wearing, which would be absurd and useless if distance was to be covered, one feels puzzled to understand.

Colonel Stewart tells us that while the "St. George" was all aback Nelson said peevishly to one of the officers, "Well, now, see what we have done.   Well, Sir, what mean you to do now?"   The other answered, "I don't exactly know, my Lord; I fear she won't do."   Nelson turned abruptly towards the cabin door, exclaiming, "Well, I am sure if you do not know what to do with her, no more do I either," and so saying he went in.   Yet he was very angry when the "Warrior," one of the ships of his squadron, touched on the Goodwins, albeit she got off without damage.

The ships brought up in the Downs, and Nelson went ashore at Deal on a visit to his old friend Admiral Lutwidge.   After the battle

of the Baltic, he saw more of Deal than pleased
him. Yet I am fond of associating Nelson with
that old town. Our leagues of foreshore submit nothing salter than Deal. The breaker
sweats in foam upon the shingle. A mile of
seaboard is filled with public-houses. You fall
over anchors and chains, and if you are not
careful you will be wound up along with the
galley-punt in the lean bars of the leaner capstan against which venerable men in tall bronzed
hats and white hair, and against which a younger
set of fellows in jerseys, monotonously press,
tramping songless round and round the shingle.

On Nelson's arrival in Yarmouth Roads with
his ships, he reported himself to Sir Hyde Parker,
who was on shore, and next morning, after break-
fasting soon after six o'clock, for he was always
up before daylight, he and Colonel Stewart went
on shore, and at eight o'clock, which Nelson
considered late for business, knocked upon Sir
Hyde's door. Nelson's scheme of war lay very
perfect in his head. His active mind abhorred
procrastination. His plan was at once to proceed to Copenhagen with such ships as he could
assemble, and there and then to insist on peace
or war. With characteristic eagerness he wanted
to be " at 'em." While at Yarmouth he wrote
to Sir Edward Berry : " I hope we shall be able,

as usual, to get so close to our enemies that our shot cannot miss their object, and that we shall again give our Northern enemies that hailstorm of bullets which is so emphatically described in the ' Naval Chronicle,' and which gives our dear country the dominion of the seas. We have it, and all the devils in Hell cannot take it from us, if our wooden walls have fair play." To Sir Hyde himself he submitted a masterly plan of attack ; and referring to the passage of the Belt, and the detachment of ten ships of three and two decks to destroy the Russian squadron at Revel, he says, " The measure may be thought bold, but I am of opinion the boldest measures are the safest." Certainly, by rapidity of action he would have anticipated the Danes in the formidable reception they were preparing to give the British. He chafed over the delay in Yarmouth Roads ; then came an Admiralty order, and the fleet put to sea.

The weather was heavy, — it usually is in the North Sea in the spring of the year. The " Invincible," seventy-four guns, Rear-Admiral Totty, went ashore and was lost. Disturbing accounts of the Danish defences had been received, and the information he had got from Mr. Vansittart and the North Sea pilots in the fleet induced Sir Hyde to choose the circuitous passage of the Great Belt. Nelson, who was all impatience, exclaimed, "Let it be by the Sound, by the Belt, or anyhow, only lose not an hour." Captain Otway succeeded in convincing Sir Hyde Parker that the Sound was the best route. The fleet was hove to that Nelson might be apprised of the reason of the change. " I don't care a damn by which passage we go so that we fight them," was Nelson's answer to Otway.

After delays which provided the Danes with ample time for rendering (as they might hope) their position impregnable, the British fleet made sail off Elsinore. The coast there is semicircular, and it was crowded with batteries. The English ships as they passed curved into a picture of beauty. Colonel Stewart speaks of the form as " truly picturesque." Finding the Swedish side silent, the fleet inclined towards that shore. The Danish batteries opened fire. The foreshore was red with the flames of guns. Every shot, however, fell short, much to the diversion of the British crews, not a man among whom was hit. A few of our leading ships fired a round or two in return, then wisely saved their powder, and the whole company of stately vessels floated onwards, with the lounging Jacks watching the " bally Scandyhoovians " futilely firing ashore.

The fleet then came to anchor, and Lord Nelson with others went in a schooner to reconnoitre the harbour and channels.   It was quickly perceived that the delay of the British to attack had been made all possible use of by the Danes. Along the northern edge of the shoals, by the Crown batteries, and in front of the harbour and arsenal, was moored a line of floating batteries, pontoons, frigate-hulks, gun-boats, every one of them bristling with guns.   The Trekroner battery had been strengthened, and the buoys which marked the navigation of the channels had been removed.   The Danes are reluctant to admit that Copenhagen was a British victory, but they will not deny that their genius as seamen rendered the British attack so formidable and perilous that, considering we had nothing but the fickle wind to depend upon, it is nothing short of marvellous that our ships should have made the passage, should have survived the deadly intricacies of the navigation, and should have placed themselves alongside the Danes' stationary hulks with scarcely less ease than had they been propelled by screws.

The Danish line of defence was four miles long.   Its approach was protected by shoals. Seventy guns were counted upon the Trekroner battery.   Of the defences, five were the hulks of men-of-war, and two were full-rigged line-of-battle ships. And off the harbour's mouth were moored four line-of-battle ships and a frigate, and the frigate and the two liners had all yards across.

Nelson attended a council of war. How was the attack to be delivered? He offered his services, and asked for ten line-of-battle ships and the whole of the smaller craft. Parker gave him two more line-of-battle ships than he demanded. During the council Stewart tells us that some of the members imagined certain difficulties in relation to the three Powers which the British were to fight in succession or all at once. Somebody represented the Russians as very formidable. Nelson paced the deck with disgust and wrath. When the Swedes were referred to as powerful and dangerous, he rounded sharply upon the speaker and said, "The more numerous the better." And when the same observation was applied to the Russians, he said, and repeated as often as the remark was made, "So much the better! I wish there were twice as many; the easier the victory, depend on it." He afterwards said that by this he referred to the want of tactical knowledge among the Northern fleets. His scheme for them was the plan he had employed at

Aboukir, and afterwards at Trafalgar. It was his intention, he said, whenever he should bring the Swedes or Russians to action, to attack their van, and so win the battle before the leeward-most of their line could come to the rescue of their comrades. He used to say, " Close with a Frenchman, but outmanœuvre a Russian."

It is told, though not confirmed by his later biographers, that on the night of the day of this council of war, Nelson in a boat personally directed the all-important service of ascertaining the course of the upper channel. His devotion was marvellous, and beautiful, and touching. Let us remember his health, the delicacy of his constitution, and think of the bitter cold of the March night upon those waters. It is idle to say that the mind is not governed by one's state of health. A man's spirit will be weakened by wounds and pain. Greatness of soul is proportioned to the power of dominating the weakness of the body and the body's appeal to that innate selfishness which is the living and active principle of life. Whenever occasion arose, Nelson's mighty mind seems to have had the power of dematerialising itself. He was as a spirit then, and heeded no more the clamours of his flesh than had they been the whispered fears of women on the eve of battle.

He shifted his flag from the " St. George " to
the " Elephant," because of the latter's lighter
draught of water. The night of the 1st of
April was dark, portentous, lowering with the
bigness of the fate of the morrow. The whole
fleet had anchored off Draco Point; the headmost of the enemy's line floated within two
miles. The Danes conceived their channel impracticable, and contented themselves with im-
proving their defences instead of firing upon the
British. Through the dusk of the night upon
the calm waters our guardboats slowly moved in
shadows, and Hardy, the gallant Hardy, even
rowed to the enemy's leading ship and sounded
round her with a pole that the dip of the lead
might not be heard.

Nelson gave a dinner-party that night. The
guests comprised Foley, Hardy, Fremantle,
Riou (" the gallant good Riou "), Admiral
Graves, and a few others. He was in high
spirits, and drank to a leading wind and to the
success of the ensuing day. When the Captains had withdrawn, Nelson was so much ex-
hausted while dictating his instructions, that his
servant, Tom Allen, an eccentric character of
the Smollett school of tars, induced him to rest
in his cot. He lay in it upon the deck, but
continued, nevertheless, to dictate. By one

o'clock the orders were completed, and a number of clerks went to work to make copies of them. All the time these clerks were writing, Nelson was shouting to them to bear a hand. In fact, it had been reported to him that the wind was becoming fair.

The ships under Nelson — twelve sail of the line and a large number of small vessels — got under way in the morning of the 2d of April; but scarcely had the signals of the different liners been made and answered, when the "Agamemnon" grounded, and shortly afterwards the "Russell" and "Bellona" touched and stuck. This was crippling the force to a degree that would have staggered most men. Nor was it the only misfortune. The "Jamaica," a frigate with a convoy of gun-boats and small craft, was swept astern by a counter current, and signalled her inability to proceed. Nevertheless, aboard the "Elephant" the signal to bear down was still kept flying. There is a stroke in the "Orders for the Attack" which is peculiarly illustrative of Nelson's character. He says, "Nos. 1, 2, 3, 4 being subdued, *which is expected to happen at an early period!*" Nothing but victory is anticipated. The inspiration of triumph makes every passage of the orders ring with the conquering note of the bugle. And now here was one of the ships, the "Agamemnon," that with the "Désirée" and another was to subdue Nos. 1, 2, 3, and 4, whose rates were seventy-four and sixty-four, while the remainder were low floating batteries — here was the "Agamemnon" ashore! The nine remaining ships anchored abreast of the Danish hulks, which bristled with ordnance and were crowded with men, harder to fight than had they been full-rigged and under way, for they were nothing but anchored fortresses, to give and receive fires till one or the other should be blown to pieces. No seamanship was wanted when the anchors had been let go — nothing but broadside after broadside, as swiftly as the guns could be made to deliver their deadly message.

The Danish commander was Fischer. His ship was the "Dannebrog," and Nelson stationed the "Elephant" abreast of her. There was uncertainty as to the depth of the water, and the action was undoubtedly prolonged on account of the distance (a cable's length) at which the contending ships were fought. I have said that no seamanship was requisite after the ships had dropped their anchors, but till *then* the manner, the judgment with which each British vessel calculated her station in those dangerous waters, and, under ever diminishing canvas, sought and secured her position, was as superb an example of seafaring skill as may be anywhere encountered in naval history. The battle was soon raging. The sheer hulks were blazing away with a resolution apparently invincible. The Danes were not Frenchmen or Spaniards. They made a splendid and a terrible enemy. Some of the decks of their ships were quickly filled with dead, and still fresh men came off from the shore and fought the guns waist-high among the corpses.

Captain Riou, observing the blank caused by the stranding of the three British ships of war, attempted with his squadron of frigates to supply the want. His ships were saved from destruction through the general signal of recall made by the Commander-in-Chief. No visible impression had been produced upon the enemy by one o'clock in the afternoon. The " Provesteen's " fire had proved deadly to the " Isis," and she must have been bombarded into fragments but for the action of the " Désirée," by whom her Danish enemy was raked. The " Holstein " and the " Zealand " were combining their broadsides in a withering fire at the " Monarch," and she was suffering severely. Signals of distress were flying on board the " Bellona " and " Russell," and the signal of disablement had been hoisted for some time on board the " Agamemnon."

It was about this time that Sir Hyde Parker, on board his flag-ship the " London," hoisted a signal for the action to cease. Nelson, during the battle, had been walking the weatherside of the quarter-deck. He was often animated in his conversation. As Colonel Stewart walked with him, a shot hammered some splinters out of the mainmast. " It is warm work," said Nelson, with a smile, " and this day may be the last to any of us at a moment." He stopped with an expression which deeply impressed the memory of his hearer. He added, " But, mark you, I would not be elsewhere for thousands." The signal-lieutenant reported the signal flying on board the " London." Nelson seemed not to heed him. The lieutenant waited for him to make a fresh turn of the deck, and said, " Shall I repeat it, my Lord ? " Nelson answered, " No ; acknowledge it." When the officer returned to the poop, Nelson said, " Is Number 16 still hoisted ? " — 16 signifying " For close action." " Yes, my Lord." " Mind you keep it so." The movement of the stump of his right arm expressed Nelson's agitation. Whenever he was worried or excited he worked his " fin," as his sailors called it. Then followed this conversation. " Do you know," said he, addressing Colonel Stewart in a quick, eager voice, "what's shown on board of the Commander-in-Chief?" " No," answered the Colonel. " Why, to leave off action," exclaimed Nelson. " Leave off action," he repeated. " Now, damn me if I do!" Then, turning to his Captain (Foley), he exclaimed, " You know, Foley, I have only one eye — I have a right to be blind sometimes," and putting the spy-glass to his blind eye he exclaimed, " I really do not see the signal." There can be no doubt whatever that this conversation took place, to the accompaniment of the thunder of the contending batteries. But to judge by what Southey, James, Dr. Scott, and others affirm, it was prearranged between Nelson and Parker that the Commander-in-Chief should hoist the signal if he thought it necessary to do so, and that Nelson should take no notice of it if he chose to continue the action. This being so, Nelson's talk and his use of the spy-glass were simply a brief dramatisation of the incident of the signal for the edification of Colonel Stewart, a soldier, for we are not to believe that British naval officers needed their spirits rallying.

The action was at its height when the " Dannebrog " was seen to be on fire. It was also observed that she had struck, but though a boat was sent to take possession, the crew meanly, inhumanely, and contrary to the usage of nations and the custom of war, fired at her. Commander Commodore Fischer had quitted the ship. Nelson speaks in the utmost contempt of this man. "In his letter he states that after he quitted the 'Dannebrog' she long contested the battle. If so, more shame for him to quit so many brave fellows. *Here* was no manœuvring: it *was* downright fighting, and it was his duty to have shown an example of firmness becoming the high trust reposed in him. He went in such a hurry, if he went before she struck, which but for his own declaration I can hardly believe, that he forgot to take his broad pendant with him; for both pendant and ensign were struck together."

Captain Mahan has coloured his fine paper in the "Century Magazine" on the battle of Copenhagen by extracts from the description of one who was a midshipman on board the "Monarch," which ship, says the American writer, lost two hundred and twenty killed and wounded, — exceeding any incurred either at the Nile or at Trafalgar. The midshipman thus proceeds: "Toward the close of the action the colonel commanding the detachment of soldiers

on board told me that the quarter-deck guns
wanted quill or tin tubes, and wanted me to send
some one, adding, his own men were too ignorant of the ship or he would have sent one of
them, I told him I knew no one who could so
well be spared as myself. He, however, objected
to my going, and as I was aware of the dreadful
slaughter which had taken place in the centre of
the ship, I was not very fond of the jaunt, but
my conscience would not let me send any other
on an errand I was afraid to undertake myself,
and away I posted towards the fore-magazine.
When I arrived on the main deck along which
I had to pass, there was *not a single man standing* the whole way from the mainmast forward, a district containing eight guns on a side,
some of which were run out ready for firing,
others lay dismounted, and others remained as
they were after recoiling. . . . I hastened down
the fore-ladder to the lower deck, and felt really
relieved to find somebody alive. I was obliged
to wait a few minutes for my cargo, and after
this pause I own I felt something like regret if
not fear as I remounted the ladder on my return.
This, however, entirely subsided when I saw the
sun shining and the old blue ensign flying as
lofty as ever. I never felt the genuine sense of
glory so completely as at that moment. I took

off my hat by an involuntary motion and gave three cheers as I jumped on to the quarter-deck. Colonel Hutchinson welcomed me at my quarters as if I had been on a hazardous enterprise and had returned in triumph; the first lieutenant also expressed great satisfaction at seeing me in such high spirits and so active.

"Our signal midshipman was bruised from head to foot with splinters in such a manner as compelled him to leave the deck. Mr. Le Vesconte, another midshipman who was my companion on the quarter-deck, and who was as cool and apparently unconcerned as usual, shared the same fate. I attended him to the lower deck, but could not prevail upon myself to set foot on the ladder to the cock-pit. I left him there to make the best of his way. As the splinters were so plentiful it may be wondered how I escaped; the fact is I did not escape entirely. When the wheel was shot away I was in a cloud, but being some little distance before the wheel I did not receive any of the larger pieces. Our first lieutenant, Mr. Yelland, had taken care to have the decks swept, and everything clean and nice before we went into action. He had dressed himself in full uniform, with his cocked hat set on square, his shirt frill stiff starched, and his cravat tied tight under his chin

as usual.   How he escaped unhurt seems wonderful.   Several times I lost sight of him in a
cloud of splinters.   As they subsided I saw first
his cocked hat emerging, then, by degrees, the
rest of his person, his face smiling, so that altogether one might imagine him dressed for his
wedding-day."   Captain Mahan justly remarks
that "we have ordinarily too little of these small
details in naval battles."   He does not know
that they are sternly repressed or contemptuously ignored by naval writers in this country.
No!   It must be: "At nineteen seconds past
one, H. M. S. 'Edgar' ported her helm
and fired a bow gun at the enemy containing
the following charge."   It is this sort of writer
who has ruined naval literature in popular
esteem.

The "Elephant," helped by the "Glatton,"
in a quarter of an hour completely silenced the
"Dannebrog," and when the smoke blew away
she was seen to be in flames, drifting through
her own line to the terror of the Danes.   The
crew were throwing themselves out of the port-
holes, and our boats rescued many of them.
She then blew up.   Not yet was the action
over, however, though many of the hulks and
other vessels of the enemy had surrendered.
But it was found that our boats when despatched

to take possession were fired on. Possibly this was due to the ignorance of the people who manned the hulks. It was quite plain to Nelson, however, that he must either send on shore and stop this irregular proceeding of firing into the boats, or send in his fireships to burn the prizes. Walking aft to the rudder-head he wrote his celebrated letter addressed —

"To the Brothers of Englishmen, the Danes.

Lord Nelson has directions to spare Denmark when no longer resisting. But if the firing is continued on the part of Denmark, Lord Nelson will be obliged to set on fire all the floating batteries he has taken, without having the power of saving the brave Danes who have defended them. Dated on board His Britannic Majesty's Ship "Elephant," Copenhagen Roads, April 2nd, 1801.

NELSON AND BRONTË,
Vice-Admiral, Under the Command of Admiral Sir Hyde Parker."

This letter was placed in an envelope. Mr. Wallis, the purser of the "Elephant," was going to seal it with a wafer, but Nelson said no. It must be properly sealed with wax, otherwise the enemy would think it was written and despatched in a hurry. Wallis sent a man below for a light; the poor fellow was killed on his way. A light was procured, and the letter sealed.   It was then sent ashore by Captain Thesiger, whose knowledge of Copenhagen and the Danish language constituted him a very fit officer to be intrusted with a flag of truce. Wallis, in recalling this incident, speaks of Nelson as dressed in a plain sort of blue greatcoat, epaulets, or gold lace.   On his breast were his several orders, and he wore a plain cocked hat. Thus we get a picture of this wonderful little man standing at the rudder-head leisurely writing and leisurely sealing a letter to the Danes.

But the might of England flush'd
To anticipate the scene ;
And her van the fleeter rush'd
O'er the deadly space between.
"Hearts of Oak!" our Captains cried ; when each gun
From its adamantine lips
Spread a death-shade round the ships
Like the hurricane eclipse
Of the sun.

Again! again! again!
And the havoc did not slack,
Till a feeble cheer the Dane
To our cheering sent us back.
Their shots along the deep slowly boom,
Then ceased, and all is wail
As they strike the shatter'd sail,
Or in conflagration pale
Light the gloom.

While the boat bearing the flag of truce was absent, the ships of the enemy's line to the eastward of the Trekroner struck. Some time after three o'clock Lindholm, returning with the flag of truce, ordered the Crown Battery to cease firing, and one of the bloodiest and fiercest actions recorded in the history of slaughter came to an end after the duration of about five hours. The Prince of Denmark's letter asked Lord Nelson for his reasons for sending his message. The answer was that the British Admiral acted only in the interests of humanity. This has been unfairly questioned by certain Danish writers, who seem to forget that Lindholm expressly wrote to Nelson that, " As to your Lordship's motives for sending a flag of truce to our Government, it can never be misconstrued, and your subsequent conduct has sufficiently shown that humanity is always the companion of true valour." There can be no doubt that Nelson was correct in stating that the Danish line of defence to the southward of the Crown Islands was much stronger and more numerous than the British. We had only five sail of seventy-fours, two sixty-fours, two fifties, and one frigate engaged. Seven shells were thrown into the Arsenal by a bomb-vessel. Niebuhr, the historian, who was in Copenhagen during the battle, says that

Nelson's conduct was absurdly undignified, and that the English ships of the line struck but could not be taken. He also says that we burnt a number of our own disabled ships, and owned in killed and wounded to two thousand men. Is Niebuhr read in this age? It may be supposed that he was in a cellar out of harm's way, or at a safe distance from shell and cannon-ball under some suburban roof; thus situated he would catch the flying rumours as they passed and make notes and history of them.

To provide against a renewal of hostilities the British fleet weighed anchor in succession. The " Monarch " grounded, but the " Ganges," by fouling, floated her. The "Defiance" and " Elephant" went ashore and stuck. The " Elephant" floated at eight that night, but Nelson, after visiting the " London," repaired on board the " St. George."

Here is presented a curious picture. The night has come down upon the waters, but all is hushed; the stillness is accentuated by memory of the thunders of the day; the wet lips of the brine sip the dusky sides of the motionless man-of-war, looming her lofty heights into shadow. Nelson sits in the cabin of the " St. George." He is alone, and writing a letter to Lady Hamilton. " My dearest friend," he says, "that same Deity who has on so many occasions protected Nelson has once more crowned his endeavours with complete success." He writes more to the same effect, then shifts his helm for a poetical cruise. Whether they are his own or the lines of somebody else I do not know; they are certainly indifferent enough to be Nelson's, whose flights of fancy make on the whole but an ill figure, though in sententious utterance and in the capacity of delivering a weighty sentiment in terse and memorable form, few were his equals. These are the lines:—

LORD NELSON TO HIS GUARDIAN ANGEL.

From my best cable tho' I'm forced to part,
I leave my Anchor in my Angel's heart;
Love, like a pilot, shall the pledge defend,
And for a prong his happiest quiver lend.

ANSWER OF LORD NELSON'S GUARDIAN ANGEL.

Go where you list, each thought of Angel's (Emma) soul
Shall follow you from Indus to the Pole;
East, west, north, south, our minds shall never part,
Your Angel's loadstone shall be Nelson's heart.
Farewell, and o'er the wide, wide sea
Bright glory's course pursue.
And adverse winds to love and me
Prove fair to fame and you:

And when the dreaded hour of battle's nigh
Your Angel's heart, which trembles at a sigh,
By your superior danger bolder grown,
Shall dauntless place itself before your own,
Happy, thrice happy, should her fond heart prove
A shield to Valour, Constancy, and Love.

" ' *St. George,*' *April 2nd,* 1801, *9 o'clock at night.   Very tired after a hard-fought battle.*"

CHAPTER IX

" ALL IN THE DOWNS "

IT was scarcely daybreak, and a bitterly cold morning. Nelson's ship, the " Elephant," had been ashore. The lookout saw a boat coming through the shadow, and as the dawn brightened she was discovered to be the gig of the " Elephant," with Lord Nelson in the stern sheets. In her he had repaired on board the " St. George," and believing the " Elephant " was still aground, had rejoined her.

His thoughts had been with his ship in which he had fought the Battle of the Baltic, and he was overjoyed at finding her afloat. He breakfasted in a hurry, and then took boat for a view of the prizes. A curious story is told by Brenton. One of the line-of-battle ships, the " Holstein," lying under the protection of the guns of the " Trekroner," had struck, but refused to acknowledge herself captured. Another ship, the " Zealand," had also struck, and about the surrender of this ship some quibble was likewise raised.   Nelson ordered one of our brigs to approach her, and then proceeded in his gig to a Danish ship within the battery to communicate with the Commodore.   Brenton affirms that Nelson had meanwhile despatched a message to Sir Hyde Parker to send Captain Otway to the " Holstein " and claim her. Otway arrived.   As the boat drove alongside the ship Otway ordered his coxswain, a daring, careless fellow, to jump aloft and bring away the pennant, whilst he (Otway) conversed with the commanding officer.   Jack sprang into the channels and trotted up the rigging without apparently exciting attention.   He hauled down the pennant, stuffed it into his bosom, and regained the boat.   Captain Otway failed to convince the Danish officer.   He pointed out, however, that the ship had struck her colours and was a prize. They agreed to refer the matter to the Danish Commodore, who in reply to Captain Otway's demand said that the ship had *not* struck her colours, that her ensign had been shot away, and that her pennant was still flying.   " Look at it, Sir ! " he said to Otway.   " Look at it yourself, Sir ! " replied Otway.   The Commodore, lifting up his eyes, saw with profound mortification that the pennant was gone !   "The ship is undoubtedly British property," he said.

With the help of a schooner, Otway cut the "Holstein's" cables, and she was towed clear of the batteries.

Meanwhile Nelson had gained the ship he had made for, and found, not Fischer, but an old West Indian acquaintance, Captain Müller, on board. He put the matter of the "Zealand" so effectively and graciously that the Danish officers not only conceded his point, but parted from him with the warmest admiration for his manner, tact, and courtesy.

Next day (April 4) submits an extraordinary picture. Nelson went ashore, accompanied by Captain Hardy and Captain Fremantle, to wait upon the Prince of Denmark. Dense crowds assembled to view him. What sort of reception was he to get? The mob seemed enraged at what they conceived his insolence in daring to land, and he was safeguarded by a strong body of troops. Some deny this, and contend that Nelson was received with acclamations. Now it is not very likely that the people of Copenhagen, after the recent hideous conflict, and after they had seen their hulks and ships in flames, or made prizes of, would greet Nelson as he stepped ashore with any sort of enthusiasm. His heroism was nothing to them. The Nile and St. Vincent made no appeal to *them*. Here was this man in a cocked hat, and an empty sleeve secured to his breast; here was this man who had put Denmark into black coolly coming ashore. " The whole town," Colonel Stewart says, " was in a state of terror, astonishment, and mourning. The oldest inhabitant had never seen a shot fired in anger at his native country."

Nelson was guarded to the Palace, dined with the Prince, then had a long talk all alone with his Royal Highness. He saw Count Bernstoff, the Danish Minister for Foreign Affairs, for a moment, and in that moment slapped his opinions into the Minister with the heat of a broadside. He told him he could not help saying he had acted a very wrong part in involving the two countries, for that our countries ought never to quarrel. Afterwards the Count gave Nelson a wide berth.

Nelson did not again land until the 9th; with him was Lindholm, who appears to have been a diplomatist of great good sense, kindness, and moderation. A crowd went with him to the Palace, but the demeanour of the people had ceased to be aggressive. The Danes were afraid of Russia: Nelson represented with unusual candour that his object in asking for a cessation of hostilities for fourteen weeks was that he might gain time to deal with the Russian fleet and then return to the Danes. A Commissioner hinted in French at a renewal of hostilities. Nelson, who had not visited France for nothing, turned to one who was with him, and exclaimed, with mingled heat and contempt, " Renew hostilities ! Tell him that we are ready at a moment, ready to bombard this very night." The Commissioner apologised.

No decision could be arrived at as to the duration of the Armistice; the matter must be referred to the Crown Prince, who held a levee in rooms which had been stripped of their furniture for fear of a bombardment. The Prince led the way upstairs to a grand dinner, and Nelson, leaning on a friend's arm, muttered in his ear, " Though I have only one eye, I see all this would burn very well." He sat on the Prince's right hand, and all was cordiality and, perhaps, revelry, though not " by night; " eventually the Prince consented to an armistice of fourteen weeks.

Writing of this battle to a friend, Nelson says, " The French have always in ridicule called us a nation of shopkeepers . . . so I hope we shall always remain, and, like other shopkeepers, if our goods are better than that of any other country, and we can afford to sell them cheaper, we must depend upon our shop being

resorted to." For this victory the King conferred on Nelson the dignity of a Viscount of
the United Kingdom of Great Britain and Ireland. There were no medals, nor did the City
of London vote its thanks. In short, though a
splendid, it was not a popular victory. The
Danes were our very good friends, in spite of
their insensate attitude in respect to the Armed
Neutrality. It was like fighting with brothers,
and triumphing over their slaughtered remains.
In our age Denmark has suffered us to cull a
sweet and tender flower from her royal garden.
We hail the princely Danish lady as mother of
our Kings to be, and this is better than bombarding Copenhagen.

Sir Hyde Parker was recalled to England,
and Nelson took his place. There is little that
lends itself to romantic colour in his proceedings
after he sailed to Revel Roads in search of the
Russian fleet. Colonel Stewart gives us a
glimpse of Nelson's life at this time. He rose
between four and five o'clock, and went to bed
about ten. Breakfast was served at six o'clock,
and sometimes it was nearer five when it was
ready. A midshipman or two were always of
the party. He never lost sight of the midshipmen. He remembered his own hopes and
dreams and fears when he was a lad at sea, and

compassion and kindness combined in his treatment of the youths. He would even during the middle watch — that is, between twelve and four in the morning — send a message of invitation to the little fellows to breakfast with him. Whilst at table he would enter into their boyish jokes, and, says Stewart, " be the most youthful of the party." He showed every consideration to his officers. " He is no sailor who ill-uses a sailor," runs the old forecastle saying, and if the excellence of a sailor is to be proportioned by his treatment of sailors, then Nelson surely was the first sailor of them all. Every officer of his ship dined with him in turn. As a host he was polite and hospitable. He invariably contrived that the business of the fleet should be despatched before eight o'clock. This gave him command of the whole day, and Colonel Stewart tells us that " the alertness which this example imparted throughout the fleet can only be understood by those who witnessed it." His principle was to keep all hands employed. The various squadrons were constantly kept on the move. " Keep them going," he used to say, " no matter how and no matter where."

Shortly before Nelson returned to England he received the instructions of his Majesty George III. to invest Rear-Admiral Graves with

the Order of the Bath. The Royal Standard
was hung over a chair raised upon a skylight on
the quarter-deck. A guard was ranged on each
hand. The chair represented the throne, and
when Nelson stepped up the ladder he made
three reverences to it. The scene was imposing.
All the captains of the fleet in full dress uniforms attended. Rear-Admiral Graves was introduced; he bowed thrice to the throne, and
once to Nelson. He then knelt, and Nelson
laid the sword upon him, accompanying this act
by a very dignified yet animated speech. He
next placed the ribbon on the new Knight's
shoulder, and the star on his left breast. The
whole fleet then fired a salute of twenty-one
guns, and the Royal Standard was hauled down.

Nelson left the Baltic in a small brig called
the " Kite," commanded by Captain Digby. He
was unwilling to take a larger craft from the
fleet. His resignation was deeply lamented by
officers and men, and a general depression
damped the spirits of the ships' companies. He
sailed on June 19 and landed at Yarmouth on
July 1. Here was a considerable voyage for a
man impatient to get home. Certainly if the
sea-officer of those days was not a good practical seaman, it was not for want of being compelled to use the sea. For months and months

a man had nothing under him but a heaving keel. Nelson was thinking of Lady Hamilton, and we need not doubt that he made Captain Digby crack on. "Topmast and t'gallant stunsails, Sir," and "Oh, yes, she'll carry that lower stunsail very comfortably. Heave the log. What is it?" "Eight, my Lord!" "Damned if those cloths have given her even half a knot." Eight knots would probably mean half a gale of wind for the brig "Kite." All acquainted with the old types of ships would know the sort of waggon *she* was. If she could look up to within six and a half points she did well. The hull of the dredger to-day ironically perpetuates the shapeliness of such a brig as Nelson washed home in from the Baltic.

On going ashore at Yarmouth he went to the house that had been called the Wrestler's Inn — it was now named Nelson's Hotel. He visited some sick and wounded men who had been brought to Yarmouth after the battle of Copenhagen; then, having lunched, he left at five o'clock for London, escorted as far as Lowestoft by a troop of cavalry. Sir William Hamilton was living in Piccadilly, and to his house Nelson repaired on his arrival in London. A party had been invited to meet him; it included the Reverend William and his wife, their son and daughter, and Captain E. T. Parker, a great favourite of Nelson. Lady Nelson was still alive; the Reverend William knew it, but this oily gentleman saw nothing in his brother's relations with Lady Hamilton to hinder him from dwelling, himself and his wife and family, under her husband's roof, and making use of her whenever opportunity gave him a chance. Nelson had no high opinion of his brother. Writing in February, 1801, he says: "My brother has a bluntness and a want of fine feelings which we are not used to; but he means nothing." And a month later he says: "Reverend Sir you will find a great bore at times; therefore he ought to amuse himself all the mornings and not always to dine with you, as Sir William may not like it."

London was hot and deserted. Sir William Hamilton was an angler. Lady Hamilton, who, of course, took complete charge of Nelson, suggested a trip to the country. They went to Box Hill and afterwards to The Bush Inn at Staines. Here Nelson wrote a letter to Lord St. Vincent, telling him he was so unwell with the pain in his stomach that he had been forced to "get again into the country." He apologises for not dining with a certain nobleman, and says that large dinners truly alarm him. The English summer

country, after weeks of shipboard and the
bloody hours of Copenhagen, must have provided such a delight as only a sailor could taste
to its innermost root. The desire of the long-
voyage mariner approaching home is to nail the
flaps of his ears to the back of his head and to
steer a straight course for the inland wood.
Nelson fished; Emma sat beside him, and, as
he had but one arm, baited the hook. They
floated upon the river Thames while Sir William
bobbed for gudgeon on the river's bank. Lord
William Gordon writes of them as Antony and
Cleopatra, and adds, —

> While you, I mean, and Henry, — in a wherry
> Are cheek by jole afloat there making merry.

Henry is Lord Nelson. Lord William clearly
had the "Henry and Emma" of Prior in his
mind.

This little holiday was made all too brief by
the call of duty. Buonaparte had this summer (1801) collected a large flotilla of flat boats
and an army at Boulogne. He did not disguise
his intention to invade England, and his candour might have proved that he meant nothing
of the sort. This country, however, was in a
state of panic. Nothing less than Lord Nelson
in person in a frigate in the Downs with his eye

on the French could soothe the general consternation.   How should we like the news in this
age that the French were collecting a great force
at Boulogne, Calais, and other places to invade
us ?   We may be quite sure we should do that
which our forefathers perhaps did not do for
want of opportunity.   I mean, we should load the
newspapers with correspondence, and every day's
issue would teem with the suggestions of naval
experts and others.   Perhaps, too, we should
realise the danger in the price of Consols.   But
our forefathers were better off than we should
be were another invasion threatened ; their merchantmen were filled with British seamen, their
convoyed fleets could bring food to their homes.
In our day the ships of our merchant navy are
undermanned with foreigners, none of whom
could be trusted if war broke out; and, as we
should have very few English seamen to fall
back upon, hundreds of merchantmen would be
laid up for lack of men.   We should be starved
by our want of foresight, and so give the enemy
a better chance of invading us.

The Commander-in-Chief in the Downs was
Nelson's old friend, Admiral Lutwidge, who
made no trouble in being superseded by Nelson.
On the 27th his flag was hoisted at Sheerness
on board the " Unité " frigate.   " To-day," says

he, writing to Lady Hamilton, "I dined with Admiral Graeme, who has also lost his right arm; and, as the Commander of the Troops has lost his leg, I expect we shall be caricatured as the *lame* defenders of England." Captain Parker, whom he regarded almost as a son, used to sit next to him at meals to cut his meat. The loss of a right arm is an inconvenient thing. Nelson makes no trouble of his personal afflictions. But a full portrait of the man should not omit even so trifling a detail as this of a friend cutting up his meat that he might dine.

His dash and spirit were instantly felt on his arrival at Sheerness. His orders comprised thirty of the ships under his command. On his way to Deal he stopped at Faversham to examine into the state of a body of men called the Sea-Fencibles. The idea of this force was due to Captain Home Popham, but he had little knowledge of the elements he sought to mould. The longshoreman was then, as he is now, a capital smuggler, a hardy lifeboatsman, very nimble in the manœuvring of his own craft, in love with that capstan of the beach against which he loafs and lounges, a great growler, and the last man in the world to trust to as a resource. In vain Nelson appealed to the Sea-Fencibles.

"Not one Frenchman," says he, "would be allowed to set his foot on British soil; it is therefore necessary that all good men should come forward at this momentous occasion to oppose the enemy, and more particularly the Sea-Fencibles, who voluntarily enrol themselves to defend their country afloat, which is the true place where Britain ought to be defended, that the horrors of war may not reach the peaceful abodes of our families." What was the issue of this and other appeals? Of two thousand six hundred Sea-Fencibles only three hundred and eighty-five offered themselves to go on board a ship. Their argument was, "Our employment will not allow us to go from our homes beyond a day or two and for actual service." As a Naval Reserve it must be admitted that Popham's Sea-Fencibles were a failure.

Nelson shifted his flag to the "Medusa" and kept watch in the Downs. It was an extremely thankless office, presently to become wofully cheerless when the rigging began to shudder with the chill of the autumnal wind. Of all picturesque sea-bits, even in this age, I know nothing more fascinating than the wide and airy field of Downs when its waters are pawed by many ships, and the white line of the Ramsgate coast gleams soft as sifted snow as it winds out of Pegwell Bay through the liquid air into an altitude of sixty or seventy feet. But in Nelson's time there survived much of that romance of the sea which has been rudely expelled from the ocean life in these days. Every ship was a picture, quaint and curious, and full of colour, brave with pennants like banners, of all varieties of mould and of divers rigs. One hears of as many as nine hundred sail bringing up in the Downs wind-bound. Nelson would sometimes witness such a sight; The French were close aboard; the tonnage that passed through the Gulls was convoyed; convoyed ships would occasionally be obliged to bring up, and there was no reason why the "Medusa" should not again and again have been surrounded by several hundred ships waiting for a slant of wind to swell their topsails for the Thames or West.

Now here is a picture for a painter: Nelson in the Downs in the "Medusa"; make the month August; his frigate in the midst of two hundred anchored merchantmen. These, with the men-of-war, would give the brush all necessary colour. In those days ships were fantastically equipped; the quaint imaginations of an earlier period (we owed much to the Dutch of the seventeenth century; their Indiamen were remarkable examples of the genius of marine decoration) still lingered as inspirations in the shipwright's yard. The stern of a ship would glow in gilt over the brine trembling from her sides, and the light of her large cabin windows would strike in spokes of fire glorifying the whole fabric, upon whose length the eye would *now* run with mingled merriment and admiration, so lofty was the poop, so depressed — yea, to the very figurehead — the bows. We would mark in her bulwarks a little grin of teeth. We would marvel at the clumsiness of her spars, yards, and rigging, yet we would admit that this very quality of clumsiness makes the picture the romantic sight we find it.

But deep interest may be found by all sea-lovers, not only in the aspect of the shipping which rode round about Nelson in the Downs, but in the various characters of the craft. You do not see the slaver now, — the long, low, black-hulled beauty with a pivoted brass gun on her forecastle, and her masts raking into a suggestion of nimble heels which affects the vision with an illusion of velocity, albeit she is at rest straining at her cable yonder. You do not see the pirate. She does not, indeed, hoist the black flag in the presence of Nelson. But that brig there, whose captain will tell you that he is

bound to the West Indies, is as surely going
a-pirating soon as the wind blows her out of the
Channel, as that she is pierced for four guns of
a side, and as that her commander has a face
that makes you think of a rat staring through a
ball of oakum, and as that her forecastle and
'tween decks are full of men who do not, in
these crowded Downs, needlessly obtrude themselves upon the general marine eye.

The French erected batteries both for guns
and mortars on each side of Boulogne, and a
line of boats, all armed, large and small, lay outside the port. These vessels were shelled by the
bombs under Nelson, but without much effect.
As early as August 3d Nelson was beginning to
suspect that the threatened invasion of our country was nothing more than a piece of bombastic
brag designed to divert attention from other
measures; for he then noticed that " these vessels anchored before this port appear to me incapable in the smoothest water of being rowed
more than one and a half [sic] per hour." He
adds: " With our present force from Dieppe
to Dunkirk certainly nothing can with impunity
leave the coast of France one mile." This is
convincing enough to a seaman. He writes,
however, with conviction next day to Adding-
ton: " I think I may venture to assure you

that the French army will not embark at Boulogne for the invasion of England."

A night scene which should be depicted by the pen of a Michael Scott unrolls itself with the panorama of Nelson's life at this time. The hour is about half-past eleven; the night is very dark. A light wind is blowing, and the decks of the " Medusa " are thrown out upon the black tapestry of the atmosphere by the dull gleams of battle lanterns. At this hour a number of boats which have been riding alongside the frigate put off. They are full of men, and are formed into four divisions commanded by Captain Philip Somerville, Captain E. T. Parker, Captain Isaac Catgrave, and Captain Robert Jones. These were the armed boats of the squadron, and they were accompanied by a division of mortar-boats. The design was to attack the French flotilla at Boulogne. Although naval historians pass lightly over this service, it was as sharp, perilous, and arduous of its kind as any you may read of. The French flotilla included brigs of from two hundred to two hundred and fifty tons, armed with from four to eight heavy long guns, eighteen, twenty-four, and even thirty-six pounders. The flats had stout bulwarks, and carried one hundred and eighty men in soldiers and seamen. They were armed with thirteen-inch mortars, twenty-four pounders, swivels, and abundance of small arms. This was a formidable flotilla for a boat to attack; and day and night the enemy was on the alert, for he knew that Nelson was near. The tide was running; the dusk was so deep that the boats lost sight of one another; the divisions dared not signal by flashes, and so, unhappily, they separated. The first division, under Captain Somerville, was carried to the eastward of Boulogne Bay. The Commander ordered the boats to cast one another off, and make for the flotilla as best they could. Just before dawn the leading boats attacked a brig lying close to the pier-head. She was carried, but she was secured by a chain, and so heavy a fire of musketry and grape-shot was opened upon our brave fellows from the shore, as well as from three luggers and a second brig, that the prize was abandoned. It was now morning; the troops were visible on the pier and upon the shore; the old town of Boulogne rose to its rampart walls, a peaceful backing for its warlike picture of harbour. It was impossible to attempt more in daylight, and with a total of eighteen killed and fifty-five wounded, the first division of boats pushed out of the bay.

Parker's division reached the flotilla before one o'clock in the morning. A large brig called the "Etna," wearing a French commodore's pendant, was instantly attacked. How splendid were those old boat-attacks of our men! Did you ever read the story of the cutting out of "La Chevrette"? It will make you proud of the blood in your veins if you are an Englishman; but it is one instance only of a thousand splendid, fearless, marvellously devoted, and heroic actions of a like sort, whether you seek for their memorials along the coast of France, or search the Mediterranean seaboard, or hunt through the maritime annals of the West Indies. The attack of Parker's people was magnificent; they gave that great British cheer which never failed to strike dismay into the heart of the foe, as has been written again and again. But by the flashes of musketry they found themselves obstructed by a very strong netting triced up to the brig's yard-arms, and it was not even in the power of British seamen to scramble over the impediment. Even while they were struggling to board, our men were fired upon by the brig's great guns and some two hundred soldiers ranged along the line of the bulwark rail. The discharge knocked our people back into the boats. The other boats of this division were also repulsed and withdrew from the scene of war, a melancholy procession, with a loss of twenty-one killed and forty-two wounded, Captain Parker being among the latter, mortally.

The efforts of the third division were equally heroic and equally futile. The fourth division, under Captain Jones, owing to the tide, could not get at the enemy, and put back to the squadron. Nelson was deeply chagrined. "My mind," he wrote to Lord St. Vincent, "suffers much more than if I had a leg shot off in this late business." In this same letter he makes an admission which should comfort the soul of the landsman: "Heavy sea, sick to death — this seasickness I shall never get over."

15

CHAPTER X.

POSSIBLY the most uncomfortable time that Nelson ever spent in his life he passed in the Downs. His worries and troubles were real and fictitious. He found Deal the coldest place in the world, and the dance of his frigate kept him ceaselessly oppressed with nausea. There he lost Captain Parker, for whom his love was as a father's for a son. The poor fellow had been desperately wounded in the attack at Boulogne. He died September 27th, and Nelson, who, in company with Admiral Lutwidge, Lord George Cavendish, and others, attended the funeral, wept during the ceremony.

He suffered also from an imaginary grievance in the behaviour of Troubridge, who was now become one of " My Lords " at the Admiralty. He seems to have believed that he was kept in the Downs entirely by Troubridge, who " has so completely prevented my ever mentioning anybody's service that I am become a cipher and he has gained a victory over Nelson's spirit. I am kept here. For what, he may be able to tell — I cannot." If Troubridge writes of him in kindness, he finds something in his language that reads like a sneer: " Troubridge writes that the weather has set in fine again ; he hopes I shall get *walks* on shore. He is, I suppose, laughing at me — but never mind."

It is rather extraordinary that Mr. Squeers' father should have written to Nelson about this time, for he tells Lady Hamilton that " It is not long ago a person from Yorkshire desired me to lend him three hundred pounds, as he was going to set up a school." This strange circumstance seems to have been overlooked by Charles Dickens in his account of Dotheboys Squeers. At the root, however, of all these complaints was a secret pining for Lady Hamilton. It is true that Sir William and Emma visited Nelson at Deal on two or three occasions, but these infrequent meetings could but increase the infatuated man's desire to be dwelling under one roof with his mistress. It is marvellous that she did not ruin his career at this juncture. Whilst he held the Downs command he bought a house without seeing it. He purchased it through Lady Hamilton, and he valued it as an estate, with plate and furniture, at twenty thousand pounds when later he wrote down a list of incomings and disbursements. The house is described by Mr. J. C. Jeaffreson as a cheery, well-built, homely villa, skirted with shrubberies, nestled in finely timbered paddocks, and within an easy drive from Hyde Park Corner. It was called Merton Place. Sir William Hamilton was astonished. "A seaman alone," he wrote to Nelson, "could have given a fine woman full powers to choose and fit up a residence for him without seeing it himself." He was finding something also in considerations of his pension to vex and humiliate him. Lords St. Vincent and Duncan, who had fought one battle apiece only, had each received a pension of three thousand pounds. Nelson, who had won two of the most glorious victories in history, to whose tactics Lord St. Vincent owed the conquest which had made a peer of him, was in receipt of no more than two thousand. He felt, and justly felt, this difference as a hardship. He fretted over it with wounded pride; nevertheless, his pension was never increased.

He was fated to endure a protracted stay in the Downs. "I pray God we may have peace, when it can be had with honour," he wrote to Hercules Ross in September, anticipating one of the late Lord Beaconsfield's original remarks, "but I fear that the scoundrel Buonaparte wants to humble us, as he has done the rest of Europe." Nevertheless, he felt the indignity of his command. Certainly this obligation of sentinelling the Narrow Seas scarcely needed the genius of a Nelson. You get a little insight into his life from his chatty letters to Lady Hamilton. He tells her he landed at Walmer, "but found Billy fast asleep, so left my card"; then he calls on Lord George Cavendish, who has gone to London; then on his old friend Lutwidge, with whom and his wife he partakes of a plain dinner, and then on board again — if, indeed, he can get on board, for often the surf runs so high that it is impossible to launch a boat.

A deep and abiding source of indignation with him was the neglect, or the refusal, of the Government to issue medals for Copenhagen. *He* had been honoured, but no testimony of appreciation beyond the thanks of Parliament had followed the splendid behaviour of our officers and men on the 2d of April, and as a true shipmate Nelson's soul was sickened by this insensibility. The City of London had made no sign, and this also galled him. He wrote indignantly that a Lord Mayor of London had said to him, "You find victories and we will find rewards," and the City of London, which exists by victories at sea, had not kept its promise.

On the 22d October he was released on leave, and straightway went to Merton, the highly idealised "cottage" which seems to have haunted his dreams, man and boy. He found a very charming house; Emma was radiant and languishing, and Sir William, pale, ill, and courteous. The place was made as rural as a sailor could wish by cocks and hens and pigs. In fact, Sir William had previously written to him: "It would make you laugh to see Emma and her mother fitting up pigstys and hencoops, and already the canal is enlivened with ducks, and the cock is strutting with his hens about the walks." Supplemented by Emma, this sort of home would be a paradise to a sailor fresh from "salt beef and honour," weary of the ceaseless motion of the deck and of the life of an anchored ship in the Downs.

On the 29th of October he took his seat in the House of Lords as a Viscount. Next day he made his maiden speech. It related to Sir James Saumarez' gallant conduct in the action with the combined fleet of the enemy off Algeziras in the preceding July. His speech was smart and full of spirit. He highly praised Sir James, and gave an account of some of his

memorable services.   Sir James was a gallant and
an able officer, but he was by no means a lov-
able character, and scarcely deserved at Nelson's
hands the warm-hearted sympathy he received.

It is extraordinary to notice that the character
of Nelson's relations with Lady Hamilton seems
to have been unsuspected even by those who
lived close to them, though how it was out of
doors we know by the King's reception and by
what Miss Cornelia Knight says.   Are we to
believe that the relations were understood and
deliberately connived at?   It is impossible to
suppose that Sir William failed to understand
what was passing under his very nose.   That
the Rev. William Nelson considered Emma
very good company for his wife merely means
that it was the Rev. William who thought so.
But how shall we reconcile old Edmund's willingness to live with his son and the Hamiltons
at Merton Place?   Yet to Merton Place he
would have gone but for his death, which happened on April 26, 1802, at Bath.   He was aged
seventy-nine, and the remains were carried to
Burnham-Thorpe for interment.   One would
wish to muse for a little on the memory and
character of a man who had Nelson for a son.
After I had written my "Life of Nelson," I
received a letter from the present Earl, in which

his Lordship informed me that I was mistaken
in my estimate of the character of the Rev. Edmund, and that he (Earl Nelson) had in his
possession several letters written by the Rev.
Edmund, exhibiting a very beautiful nature and
disposition. I cannot but repeat, however, what
I have before said, that Nelson's father was a
man of a cold, formal, and insipid piety, whose
expression you cannot follow in his published
correspondence without displeasure and often
disgust. But, as I have said, his son loved,
honoured, and liberally cherished him to the
end.

While he was on shore on leave, Nelson
made a journey into Wales. The inevitable
Hamiltons accompanied him, and with him
went the Rev. William Nelson, his wife and
son. They visited Blenheim, and all will regret
to learn that they were most unequivocally
snubbed. The Duke of Marlborough declined
to receive them; indeed, they might have been
a set of cockney excursionists. The Duke, on
hearing that they were in his grounds, was good
enough to send some refreshments out to them;
but they refused to partake of his gracious hospitality. One of this party had been British
Ambassador at Naples, and another was the
greatest naval hero the world had ever produced!

It is said that the Duke was a very shy man. An apology has been made for him by suggesting the absence of the usual ceremonies of introductory etiquette. It is more than probable, however, as is suggested by the writer of the "Memoirs of Lady Hamilton," that the party were declined admittance because the ladies of the Marlborough family did not desire the honour of Lady Hamilton's acquaintance. This, indeed, makes a strange picture in Nelson's life. To think of our beloved hero inhospitably repulsed from the lordly pile which memorialises the exploits of a great warrior by land! What was in his mind whilst he contrasted the Palace of Blenheim with its miles of rich estate with his own little home of Merton Place? Is it better to be a great General in this maritime country than a great Admiral? It is earnestly to be hoped that Nelson did not long linger within the precincts of that ducal building. Everywhere else, however, he met with all the honour he deserved. They rang the bells of the churches. Crowds hurrahed themselves hoarse. Bands of music greeted him. Guns were fired, and the militia turned out. At Swansea he was dragged in triumph by a body of sailors. Floral arches were erected; the cities bestowed their freedoms upon him. At Monmouth he made a speech, the concluding sentences of which are well worth transcribing : " In my own person I have received an overflowing measure of the nation's gratitude — far more than I ever merited or expected ; because the same success would have crowned the efforts of any other British Admiral who had under his command such distinguished officers and such gallant crews. And here let me impress it on the mind of every officer in the Service that to whatever quarter of the globe he may be destined, whether to the East or West Indies, to Africa or America, the eyes of his countrymen are upon him, and so long as public men in public stations exert themselves in those situations to fulfil the duty demanded from them by the public, they will always find the British nation ready to heap upon them the utmost extent of its gratitude and its applause."

These are words which sound as trumpet tones through the years, and it is well in our days of peace that we should sometimes look back and hear and see what those great sailors were doing and saying in those red and dreadful times of war.

Sir William Hamilton departed this life on the 6th of April, 1803. Nelson and Emma had sat up together for six nights by the bedside of the sick man, who died holding his wife's and

Nelson's hands.   It never will be credited that
Sir William was ignorant of his wife's infidelity,
yet he expressly says in a remarkable letter: " I
well know the purity of Lord Nelson's friendship for Emma and me."   Nelson made much
of this loss in his correspondence and lamented
it most strenuously.   Lady Hamilton was not
to be outdone.   She poses thus upon her husband's remains: " April 6. — Unhappy day for
the forlorn Emma.   Ten minutes past ten, dear,
blessed Sir William left me."

Not for long, however, was Nelson to enjoy
the society of the widow.   On May 16 he was
appointed Commander-in-Chief of the Mediterranean.   On that date war was declared, and
his instructions were to proceed to Toulon and
deal with the ships of the enemy as he could.
He was also to keep an eye on the Spaniard
and the Dutch at sea, and to prevent Spanish
ships of war from combining with French or
Dutch squadrons.   On the 18th of May he
hoisted his flag on board the " Victory " at Spithead.   His characteristic eagerness is again
shown.   A despatch from Portsmouth, dated
May 20, stated that such was " the anxiety of
Lord Nelson to embark, that yesterday, to
every one who spoke to him of his sailing he
said, ' I cannot before to-morrow, and that's

an age.' This morning, before ten o'clock, his Lordship went off in a heavy shower of rain, and sailed with a northerly wind."

He was now to enter upon one of the most tedious of all the services that naval warfare provided for the sailor in the days of tacks and sheets. He was to watch Toulon. He was to fight the French ships if they came out. But they would not come out, and so he had to keep on watching Toulon. His spell of work ran into eighteen months. It is impossible to describe the tediousness of it, though Collingwood's term of devoted service after Trafalgar ran into five years — that is, from 1805 to 1810, in which year he died at sea while going home. It was constantly blowing Levanters, and whenever the sea ran high Nelson was sick. He found it hard to imagine what the enemy intended to do. Sometimes he thought that they would try to take Sicily before pushing on to Egypt; sometimes that the fleet would go direct to cover the army across the Morea; sometimes that the enemy was bound outside the Mediterranean. This spell of watching the French is memorable for the excellent health enjoyed throughout by the several ships' companies, — wholly due to the sanitary victualling measures of Nelson. When ships watched ports they did not heave to, but sailed up and down in front of them. At regular intervals, therefore, the vessels went about. The beat of a pendulum could not be more monotonous. As pictures, the line-of-battle ships would look very stately, swelling white and lofty ; a line-of-battle ship in "stays" made a grand figure ; she floated round in grandeur into the wind. This might be very well for once or twice, but eighteen months of it ! with gale after gale which blew the ships out of sight of land, reduced them to storm-canvas and drove them sagging to leeward with struck topgallant masts ! Nor were the ships a credit to the country. Nelson wrote to the Duke of Clarence that he had the happiness to command the finest squadron in the world : "Victory," "Kent," "Superb," "Triumph," "Belle Isle," and "Renown." But to others he told the truth. "To watch the French," he says, "I must be at sea, and if at sea must have bad weather ; and if the ships are not fit to stand bad weather they are useless. I do not say much, but I do not believe that Lord St. Vincent would have kept the sea with such ships."

A poor-hearted coxcomb, one La Touche Tréville, was the French Admiral at Toulon. Like most cowards, this man was a liar. He

caused a statement to be printed in the " Mon-
iteur" to the effect that he had sailed out of
port on the 14th of June and put the English
Admiral to flight.   Nelson bitterly resented this
infamous fabrication.   How could he answer
such a fellow?   " I do assure you, Sir," he
wrote to the Secretary of the Admiralty, " that
I know not what to say except by a flat contradiction, for if my character is not established by
this time for not being apt to run away, 't is not
worth my time to attempt to put the world
right."   He writes to others that if he gets hold
of La Touche he will make him eat his letter.
The French Admiral, however, cheated Nelson
of his revenge by dying a few weeks after the
lie had been published.   The French papers,
with unconscious irony, stated that he died in
consequence of walking so often up to the signal-
post upon Sepet to watch the British.   " He
has gone," wrote Nelson, " and all his lies with
him."

The Rev. Dr. Scott enables us to look a little
closely into what may be termed the below-
deck life of Nelson.   The Admiral had met
Scott in the Mediterranean ; the chaplain was
afterwards up in the Baltic and helped Nelson
in the arrangement of the celebrated Convention
of Copenhagen.   He was now Chaplain of the

"Victory," and he was one of the few who min-
istered to Nelson when he lay dying. Scott was
a fine linguist, and Nelson put him to wade
through countless trifling foreign pamphlets, his
idea being that no man ever put his hand to
paper without having some information or theory to deliver worth attention.   So side by side
Nelson and the Chaplain would sit in the
Admiral's cabin toiling through interminable
papers. They occupied two black leather arm-
chairs furnished with capacious pockets, and
sometimes, when Scott was weary of translating,
he would contrive to smuggle into one of these
pockets, unobserved by Nelson, a bundle of
unopened private letters found in prize ships.
These chairs with an ottoman, when lashed together, formed a bed on which Nelson often
slept. Scott indicates in Nelson a quality of
mind which one would not suspect from his correspondence or from such speech as is placed in
his mouth by his biographers. It is the dry,
arch quality that Swift enjoyed in Stella, the disposition to encourage a man to talk, and if he
should prove a blockhead, to sink him deeper
in his own absurdity. Scott, though a very good
man, may be suspected of vanity, and Nelson
appears to have diverted himself with trotting
the parson out before company. " Often after

dinner he would lead the Doctor into arguments on literature, politics, Spanish language, naval affairs, and even invite him to deliver a lecture on navigation. The Doctor took him seriously, to the great entertainment of Captain Hardy, and the officers who might be present."

In Dr. Scott's Life a good story is told of Nelson. A midshipman's servant fell overboard, and the midshipman to whom the fellow belonged shot after him. Nelson was highly delighted by this act of bravery, and when the pair had been hauled on deck, he called the streaming midshipman aft and made him lieutenant. A number of midshipmen were on deck, and the cheer they gave in honour of their messmate caught Lord Nelson's ear. He seemed to find something significant in it, and, lifting his hand for silence, he turned to the crowd of middies, and said, with a good-natured smile on his face: "Stop, young gentlemen! Mr. Flin has done a gallant thing to-day — and he has done many gallant things before — for which he has got his reward. But mind, I'll have no more making lieutenants for servants falling overboard." The quiet humour of this is worthy of Elia.

An instance of Nelson's liberality and kindness of heart may here be given. He took a

large land force afloat in his chase of the French
after his arrival at the West Indies, and learning
that the sailor got one pound of meat per day,
whilst the allowance to the soldier was only
three-quarters of a pound, he gave orders that
so long as the men were under his command
the rations to the services should be made
equal.

Meanwhile Nelson kept his fleet remarkably
healthy, and in fine order, as he himself ex-
presses it, "to give the French a dressing."
The weather was constantly bad. He wrote to
Lady Hamilton on October 18 that since
September 1 they had not had four fine days,
"and," he adds, "if the French do not come
out soon I fear some of my ships will cry out."
After La Touche's death Rear Admiral Duma-
noir took command of the French fleet; he
was shortly afterwards replaced by Villeneuve.
Nevertheless, the Frenchmen did not put to sea
until Jan. 18, 1805. When the news reached
Nelson he was with his ships at Maddalena.
The enemy was said to have been steering
south. Nelson went to Egypt. He did not
find the Frenchmen there, and returned. On
his arrival at Malta he heard that the enemy
had put back to Toulon with many of their
ships crippled.

They sailed again, however, from Toulon on March 30, but it was not until May 11 that Nelson, who had gathered that the enemy's combined fleet amounted to eighteen sail of the line, and that it had gone direct for the West Indies, went in pursuit.

Strange to observe in naval history how it is always the British who are chasing the French. A small squadron flying the British flag locks up in port a big fleet flying the tricolour. In vain the British coquette with the enemy. They pretend to go away; they pretend to run away; they endeavour to coax Crapeau out by cunning exhibitions of very inferior strength. To no purpose. When Johnny does creep forth he has taken care to see that the road is clear. How do French historians relate these matters in the little histories of France which they write for school-boys? Possibly they cite such authorities as Mr. La Touche Tréville.

Here now was Nelson in full pursuit of the French fleet across the wide Atlantic to the West Indies. The enemy's force consisted of eighteen ships of the line, and, for all Nelson knew the force might be augmented to twenty-eight or thirty when the Frenchmen reached their destination. Nelson's squadron was composed of ten sail of the line, and three frigates.

He had got some news of Cadiz by speaking the "Louisa" of Baltimore, which sailed from the Spanish port on May 2. Peter Billings, the Master, told Nelson of the sailing of five Spanish line-of-battle ships, a French eighty-gun ship, and some smaller craft. Also he spoke of eleven French sail of the line and four frigates appearing off Cadiz, and of a Spanish line-of-battle ship of great value having touched the ground on going out. Billings talked of three thousand Spanish troops, and of the confusion that attended their embarkation. He said that the Spaniards could not get their ships to sea without great trouble. He reported that provisions were plentiful and cheap, but seamen were scarce, and those they had were most reluctant to serve. Truly might Nelson write to the Secretary of the Admiralty : " It will not be fancied I am here on a party of pleasure running after eighteen sail of the line with ten, and that to the West Indies."

On the squadron's arrival at the islands, the hunt was to begin. Where were the French ? At Barbadoes, Nelson was informed that General Brereton had received information that twenty-eight sail of the enemy's fleet had been sighted off St. Lucia heading south. Upon this intelligence Nelson relied, though he afterwards had reason to curse it, as, in fact, in many of his letters he did curse it. He proceeded to Tobago, thence to Trinidad, thence to Grenada, and here he learnt that the enemy had been seen standing to the northwards, and that he had captured a convoy of fourteen sail of sugar-loaded ships. He sailed to Montserrat, anchored at St. John's, Antigua, to land two thousand troops, that Lieutenant-General Sir William Myers had embarked, himself in command of them; and this done, judging now that the combined fleet were making for Europe, he sailed on his return journey.

This is a service very easily recited; but the arduousness, the devotion of it, the marvellous spirit which animated a little squadron of ten or twelve ships to hunt after twenty-eight or thirty huge sail of the line,—how is this to be expressed? One must endeavour to remember there was no steam in those times. Ships had to snatch propulsion as best they could out of the antagonism of head winds, or that most irritating condition of the life of the sailing-ship, the calm and the catspaw. It is quite certain that Nelson meant to attack the enemy, let him be in what force he might. He is reported to have said, speaking without reserve to some of his Captains: " Do not imagine I am one of those hot-brained people who fight at immense disadvantage without an adequate object.   My object is partly gained "— he meant that he had driven the enemy from the West Indies.   "If we meet them we shall find them no less than eighteen, I should rather think twenty, sail of the line, and therefore do not be surprised if I should not follow them immediately.   We won't part without a battle."   Nelson was not the man to pursue with the idea of evading an enemy.   "Our battle," he tells the Duke of Clarence, "most probably would have been fought on the spot where the brave Rodney beat De Grasse."

The squadron sailed slowly across the Atlantic, keeping a bright look-out for the Frenchmen and the Spaniards.   Slow the passage was, according to the reckoning of these times,—an average of a little more than a hundred miles a day. You see the chafing, eager, ardent mind of the man in this brief extract of his private diary dated June 21, 1805 : "Midnight, nearly calm, saw three planks, which I think came from the French fleet.   Very miserable, which is very foolish." It is midnight, and he is on the look-out. There may be a corner of moon in the sky; or perhaps in the gleams of the phosphorus clouding the brow of the swell with golden lustre, he is able to distinguish the three planks.   Nearly calm! This is death to his irritable spirit. How sickening to him must be the hollow flap of the canvas as it beats the masts, raising a musketry of reef-points! Many a yarn could the old "Victory," as she lies off Portsmouth, spin (in the dialect of creaking timbers) of this wonderful pursuit of the French and Spanish by a few British ships of war across the Atlantic and back. Nelson's impatience, his "Jump aloft, young gentleman, and report anything in sight," the straining of his eye round the horizon, the hope that lighted up his face even when a pinion of sail was reported; this and very much more than this, could the old "Victory" whisper to a listener who knows how to interpret the language of ships.

Nelson anchored at Gibraltar on July 19, and on the 20th he made this entry in his private diary: "I went on shore for the first time since the 16th June, 1803, and from having my foot out of the 'Victory' two years wanting ten days."

CHAPTER XI

NELSON sailed from Gibraltar with his squadron, and off Ushant joined the Channel fleet under Cornwallis. On the same day he sailed for Spithead in company with the " Superb," and then struck his flag and went to Merton. Here he found repose after his arduous sea-toil, and happiness in the company of Lady Hamilton and his daughter Horatia. He seemed little disposed to move about in paying visits. He declined an invitation to Fonthill, the residence of William Beckford; his excuse was that all his family were with him and that the period of his stay was very uncertain. His family consisted of his brother William, Mrs. William, and their children, Horace and Charlotte (afterwards Lady Bridport), the Boltons, one of whom, Mr. Thomas Bolton, afterwards became second Earl Nelson, the Matchams, and Lady Hamilton. There never was so good and loyal a relative as Nelson. He was constantly endeavouring to assist one connection or another.

It is told of Nelson that one morning, walking in the grounds at Merton with Admiral Sir Richard Keats, and talking on Naval matters, the hero said to his friend : " No day can be long enough to arrange a couple of fleets and fight a decisive battle according to the old system. When we meet them, for meet them we shall, I 'll tell you how I shall fight them. I shall form the Fleet into three Divisions in three Lines. One Division shall be composed of twelve or fourteen of the fastest two-decked Ships, which I shall always keep to windward, or in a situation of advantage ; and I shall put them under an officer who I am sure will employ them in the manner I wish if possible. I consider it will always be in my power to throw them into battle in any part I may choose, but if circumstances prevent their being carried against the enemy where I desire, I shall feel certain he will employ them effectually, and perhaps in a more advantageous manner than if he could have followed my orders. With the remaining part of the Fleet formed in two lines, I shall go at them at once, if I can, about one third of their Line from their leading ship. What do you think of it ? "   Keats felt the question required consideration. Nelson observing that he paused, exclaimed, "But I'll tell you what I think of it. I think it will surprise and confound the enemy. It will bring forward a pell-mell battle, and that is what I want." This story is preserved by Nicolas.

At last came the 2d of September, on which day Captain Blackwood, of the "Euryalus," arrived at the Admiralty with intelligence that the Combined Fleets had put into Cadiz. As early as five o'clock in the morning Blackwood presented himself at Merton, and found Nelson up and dressed. On seeing Captain Blackwood, Nelson exclaimed, "I am sure you bring me news of the French and Spanish Fleets, and I think I shall yet have to beat them." Lady Hamilton, who dictated a book about Nelson to a Mr. Harrison, would have us believe that Nelson received the news of the Franco-Spanish fleet with indifference. Even Southey declares that he asserted it was nothing to him. "'Let the man trudge it who has lost his budget,'" Emma makes Nelson gaily observe. This insensibility, to be sure, is highly consistent with the memorable and marvellous pursuit he was fresh from! But Emma is very minute. She bids us observe that he was pacing one of the walks of Merton garden, which he always called the quarter-deck, when she told him she perceived he was low and uneasy. He answered with a smile, "No, I am as happy as possible. I am surrounded by my family. My health has improved since I have been at home, and I would not give a sixpence to call the King my uncle." "I do not believe what you say," exclaimed Emma. "I will tell you what is the matter with you. You are longing to get at those French and Spanish fleets which you consider as your own property, and you will be miserable if any other man but yourself did the business." She then told him to go and offer his services, assured him that they would be accepted, and that he would have a glorious victory. He looked at her for some moments (so she says), and with tears in his eyes — Nelson weeping on such an occasion is a stroke worthy of Emma — he exclaimed: "Brave Emma, good Emma! If there were more Emmas there would be more Nelsons."

This trash signifies that had Lady Hamilton turned her attention to fiction she might have written novels as good as Mrs. Gore's or Lady Blessington's. Happily, the impudent courtesan's lies availed her nothing.

Emma or no Emma, Nelson received orders to resume the command of the Mediterranean fleet, and on the night of Friday, September 13, he left Merton for ever. He made this entry in his private diary: " At half-past ten drove from dear, dear Merton, where I left all which I could hold dear in this world to go to serve my King and country. May the great God, whom I adore, enable me to fulfil the expectations of my country; and if it is His good pleasure that I should return, my thanks will never cease being offered up to the throne of His mercy. If it is His good providence to cut short my days upon earth, I bow with the greatest submission, relying that He will protect those so dear to me that I may leave behind. His will be done. Amen, amen, amen."

No man can go forth to fight for his country without gloomy forebodings, not perhaps as to the issue of the struggle, but as to whether he shall live to return home. Sir Harris Nicolas considers that Nelson's mind was strongly impressed with the probability that he would never return alive. It is stated that before he left London he called upon his upholsterer in Brewer Street, where the coffin presented to him by Captain Hallowell had been sent, and requested that an attestation of its identity should be engraved on the lid, for, he said, " I think it highly probable that I may want it on my return."

He was greatly moved on leaving Merton. About ten at night, a few minutes before quitting his home, he went to his child's room and said a prayer over her. He then bade goodbye to Lady Hamilton, entered the chaise, and reached Portsmouth next day. It is very evident that Nelson was not a superstitious man, or he certainly would not have chosen a Friday, and a 13th of the month for his departure, when by lingering another hour and a half he could have made it Saturday the 14th.

All who have any knowledge of the life of Nelson will remember that wonderful scene of departure on the shore before he pushed off in his boat. He had hoped to elude the crowd by quitting the George Inn through a back way, but they were on the beach waiting; they formed in procession after him. Southey tells us that many were in tears, and many knelt down before him and blessed him as he passed. When his barge pushed off the people wept and cheered, and wept again. Nelson answered by waving his hat. Some waded into the water by the side of his boat. It was an extraordinary and pathetic picture. But then Southey has truly said, " England has had many heroes, but never one who so entirely possessed the love of his fellow-countrymen as Nelson. All men knew that his heart was as humane as it was fearless; that there was not in his nature the slightest alloy of selfishness or cupidity; but that with perfect and entire devotion he served his country with all his heart, and with all his soul, and with all his strength; and therefore they loved him as truly and as fervently as he loved England."

He was deeply touched by this demonstration of popular affection, and turning to Captain Hardy, exclaimed, "I had their huzzas before — I have their hearts now."

He sailed on the 15th in the "Victory" in company with the "Euryalus," and on the 28th joined the fleet off Cadiz under Vice-Admiral Collingwood. He requested that no salute should be fired, and that no colour should be hoisted, as it was undesirable to proclaim to the enemy the news of every ship which joined the fleet. He was received with the greatest enthusiasm, from Collingwood down to the loblolli-boy. He communicated with the commanders on the day after his arrival, and explained to them what he termed the "Nelson touch." "It was like an electric shock," he writes to Emma; "some shed tears, all approved. It was new, it was singular, it was simple, and from Admirals downwards it was repeated. 'It must succeed if ever they will allow us to get at them.'"

His presence was doubly welcome; it brought with it a social sunshine into the fleet. The Captains dined with him; the restraints which they had been made to feel under Collingwood vanished. I have the profoundest admiration for Lord Collingwood, but it must be admitted that the austerity and reserve of his character were not conducive to social intercourse and happiness. He was wrapped up in his duty and in his thoughts of his wife and children. Yet it is strange that the very charge which his Captains preferred against him, — his want of hospitality, his seeming incapacity of good-fellowship, — he had himself brought with great emphasis against Lord St. Vincent when he was serving under that Admiral. This I have pointed out in my Life of Collingwood.

Nelson tells us that the officers who came on board to welome his return forgot his rank as Commander-in-Chief in the enthusiasm with which they greeted him. The plan of attack which he laid before the commanders he had thought out before he left England, for we are told that whilst dining with his friend Lord Sidmouth, he drew out his plan upon a small table, saying, " I shall attack in two lines, led by myself and Collingwood, and I am confident I shall capture either their van and centre or their centre and rear." In one respect the fleet was ill-furnished; Nelson had but two frigates (so he writes on the 5th October) to watch the enemy in Cadiz, and he declares that a fleet thus watching should never be with less than eight frigates and three good, fast-sailing brigs. By the 11th, however, he had five frigates, a brig, and a schooner on this service.

The enemy showed no disposition to move. That the Combined Fleet would be obliged to come out sooner or later was certain; Collingwood had taken great care to intercept all supplies of provisions, and the enemy must either fight or starve.

Nelson's habits of life at this period have been recorded by the surgeon of the "Victory," Beatty. The merest trifles are of interest when they relate to Nelson. Beatty tells us that the hero had rid himself of the gout by abstaining for the space of nearly two years from animal food and wine, and all other fermented drink; during this space he was a vegetarian and drank only milk and water. Early in life, we are told, he attributed scurvy to salt, and left it off, and never afterwards took it with his food. He would walk the deck for six or seven hours a day. He

rose almost habitually shortly after daybreak.
He breakfasted in summer at six, and at seven
in winter, and dined at about half-past two.
These particulars, let it be understood, refer to
the period immediately preceding Trafalgar.
Eight or nine officers of the different ships
usually formed his company at table. He still
continued very sparing in his diet; his dinner
was often composed of the liver and wing of a
fowl and a small plate of macaroni. He drank
champagne, never, however, exceeding four
glasses. He was very careless of his health.
He took no pains to guard against wet or the
night air, wore only a thin greatcoat, and would
sit in wet clothes, saying that his leather waistcoat protected him. He seldom wore boots,
and his feet were often damp; and his method
of drying them was by throwing off his shoes
and walking on the carpet in his stockings.
This he did to save his servant trouble, for, be
it remembered, he had but one arm, and could
not help himself in all offices requiring the use
of two hands.[1]

Twelve of the ships of the Combined Fleet
floated out of Cadiz on Saturday, the 19th of
October. The rest did not succeed in quitting
the harbour owing to the scantiness of the wind.

[1] All this we owe to Dr. Beatty.

Blackwood, on board the " Euryalus," signalled
that " The enemy are coming out of port."
The " Victory," with the main body of the fleet,
was some leagues distant. The signal was flown
for a general chase south-east. It was not, however, until daylight next morning that the remainder of the Franco-Spanish fleet weighed
and put to sea. Some say that Villeneuve
formed his fleet in five columns ; others, in
three. There were thirty-three ships in all,
with smaller vessels. Among them was the
huge " Trinidad," and the sight they presented
on the morning of Trafalgar was that of a sort
of crescent, so that, to employ Collingwood's
description, " In leading down to their centre,
I had both their van and rear abaft the
beam."

Early in the morning of the ever memorable
21st of October the " Victory " made the signal
to " Form the order of sailing in two columns."
She took out all reefs, set royals and stunsails,
and cleared for action. Nelson was on deck
soon after dawn. He was dressed in his Admiral's frock-coat, on the left breast of which were
four stars of different orders. He was without
his sword, though it had been placed ready for
him on his table. This description of Nelson's
dress was confirmed by Captain Sir George

Westphal, who was a midshipman in the "Victory." While the two divisions of ships were sailing towards the Combined Fleets — the lee line led by Collingwood in the "Royal Sovereign," the weather line led by Nelson in the "Victory" — the hero gave particular directions for carefully removing the portrait of Lady Hamilton from his cabin. "Take care of my guardian angel," he said, and then went below and wrote the following historic prayer —

Monday, October 21st, 1805.

At daylight saw the Enemy's Combined Fleet from East to E.S.E.; bore away; made the signal for Order of Sailing, and to Prepare for Battle; the Enemy with their heads to the Southward: at seven the Enemy wearing in succession. May the Great God, whom I worship, grant to my Country, and for the benefit of Europe in general, a great and glorious Victory; and may no misconduct in any one tarnish it; and may humanity after Victory be the predominant feature in the British Fleet. For myself individually, I commit my life to Him who made me, and may His blessing light upon my endeavours for serving my country faithfully. To Him I resign myself and the just cause which is entrusted to me to defend. Amen. Amen. Amen.

An anecdote in connection with this prayer is interesting. John Pasco acted as signal-lieutenant of the "Victory." Whilst the fleet was sailing towards the French and Spanish ships Pasco went below to make a report and submit a grievance to Nelson. He entered the cabin and discovered Nelson on his knees writing. He was composing the prayer I have just transcribed. Pasco waited till he rose, and then communicated some report of the deck, but felt himself unable to represent any troubles of his own at such a moment.

"The day is fine, the sight, of course, beautiful," Blackwood had written to his wife on the 19th, referring to the Combined Fleets which were coming out of Cadiz. The sight was equally beautiful, but grand and tremendous, with all tragic and momentous significance on this morning of the 21st. The enemy's ships floated like the marble shapes of cathedrals: they shone in the sun with the lights and splendour of the iceberg. There was little wind, scarce enough to keep their topgallant sails shuddering as they lay on the port tack with their heads to the north, and Cadiz snug under their lee. The Atlantic swell rolled into the shoals, barely wrinkled by the faint blue breathings of that October morning. But the British ships gathered an impulse from the subtle, irresistible respiration of the deep, and their canvas swelled as they bowed with royal stateliness forward on the send of the following folds.

The "Royal Sovereign," with her stunsails making a light in the sea beside her, was ahead of the foremost of the ships by twenty minutes. Collingwood, we are told by Hercules Robinson, a midshipman on board the "Euryalus," gravely paced the deck munching an apple. They called him "dear old Cuddie." What a heart of oak was that! What a splendid set of fellows filled his 'tweendecks! Just before that distant ship awoke the first low thunders of Trafalgar, a signal was made on board the "Victory." "His Lordship came to me on the poop," says Pasco, "and after ordering certain signals to be made, about a quarter to noon, he said: 'Mr. Pasco, I wish to say to the Fleet, ENGLAND CONFIDES THAT EVERY MAN WILL DO HIS DUTY. And,' he added, 'you must be quick, for I have one more to make, which is for *Close Action.*' I replied: 'If your Lordship will permit me to substitute *expects* for *confides*, the signal will soon be completed, because the word *expects* is in the vocabulary, and *confides* must be spelt.' His Lordship replied in haste and with seeming satisfaction, 'That will do, Pasco; make it directly.'" Thus was hoisted the immortal signal. They say the

crews cheered when its import was communicated. A few ships of the van answered it, and
then was hoisted at the mizzen-royal masthead
Nelson's favourite signal for Close Action —
No. 16.

The foe submitted a brave, bristling, tremendous picture — thrity-three Leviathans, the
Spaniards with crosses dangling at their spanker-
boom ends. And towering in the thick of that
crescent-like huddle lay the "Trinidad," of four
rows of teeth and filled with breathless men and
a number of priests. Shortly after the memorable signal had been made aboard the "Victory,"
a French ship, the "Fougueux," lying astern of
the "Santa Ana," sent a shot at the "Royal
Sovereign." Then it was that the three British
Admirals hoisted their respective flags, and
every ship seized[1] a Union Jack to her maintopmast stay, and another to her fore-topgallant
stay. Then it was, too, that, with one exception,
the Admirals of the Combined Fleets hoisted
their ensigns.

The picture of the "Royal Sovereign" alone
in action was sublime, was magnificent, but
whether it was war or not others must pronounce. Had it fallen a dead calm so as to
prevent our ships from approaching the enemy,

---

[1] To seize is to attach, to secure.

her fate must have been sealed; she must have been bombarded into staves, for she not only had the "Santa Ana" (which, by the way, suffered frightfully from Collingwood's first broadside) to contend with; ahead lay the "San Leandro;" the "Fougueux" raked her astern, and close aboard on the starboard bow and quarter lay the two monsters, "San Justa" and "Indomptable." These ships blazed their roaring artillery into the devoted British liner. "Rotherham," exclaimed Collingwood at this time to his Captain, "what would Nelson give to be here!" And Nelson, watching the glorious sight, exclaimed, "See how that noble fellow Collingwood carries his ship into action!"

Every glass, James tells us, on board the "Victory" was employed to discover the flag of the French Commander-in-Chief. Nelson's desire was to get at Villeneuve. All this while the "Victory" was slowly floating to within gunshot of the enemy's line irregularly followed by the ships of the division she led. About twenty minutes after the "Fougueux" had fired at the "Royal Sovereign" the "Bucentaure" let fly a shot at the "Victory." It fell short. A second shot dropped alongside. At last a fifth or sixth shot pierced the main-topgallant sail. "A minute or two of awful silence ensued," says James. Then in a mighty shock of thunder nearly the whole of the weathermost ships of the enemy blazed their great ordnance at the "Victory." Almost never before had such a fire been directed at a single ship. She kept silent, and continued to float onwards at the rate of about a knot.

Nelson's tactics were these. The "Victory" was to break through the enemy's line at about his tenth ship. This being done, some nine or ten of the enemy's ships to leeward were rendered useless; they had no steam to propel them to the help of their friends; the air was so light that it was impossible they could have had way enough upon them to tack, and the battle would have been decided by the time they wore. Nelson, thus, by his plan of attack, created for his twenty-seven ships a stronger force than the Combined Fleets could oppose to him, thirty-three as they were.

Shortly after the "Victory" fired her first fatal broadside, the ships astern of the British leaders broke through the Franco-Spanish line in all parts, and, to quote Collingwood, " engaged the enemy at the muzzles of their guns." James tells us that when the French and Spanish ships perceived that the "Victory" was about to follow the example of the " Royal Sovereign," "they closed like a forest." This is difficult to realise, seeing that he informs us that by this time the wind had gradually died away to a mere breath, and that the "Victory" owed such motion as she had to the impulse of the swell.

A shot passed between Nelson and Hardy as they paced the deck. They stopped and looked at each other, each supposing the other wounded. Nelson then smiled and said : " This is too warm work, Hardy, to last long," and he added that he had never in all his experience witnessed more cool courage than was being displayed by the "Victory's" crew. Warm work it was! Every ship that could point a gun at the "Victory" was firing at her. She floated under the stern of the "Bucentaure," and smashed a broadside into the Frenchman's cabin windows. She was receiving at this time the direct fire of the "Neptune" and the "Redoutable." She then fell foul of the latter ship. The scene now becomes a lurid and tremendous picture. Masts come crashing from aloft; canvas and bulwarks are riddled into the appearance of gratings, ship falls upon ship, and they engage so close that the men who fight the guns are almost suffocated by the black and filthy vomitings. What were the sensations of the captains

in command of those ships which Nelson's tactics had as effectually disabled as if they had
been sunk or burnt? The British attack was
irresistible. There was no virtue in the spirit
of the Spaniard or the Frenchman to oppose
that terrific shock of war. We were fighting for
peace, we were fighting to annihilate the enemy
that peace might be assured. Prize-money was
a quite secondary consideration; those devils
alongside were to be subdued at the cost of
extermination, as Nelson said, and he cared not
whether they floated or sank so long as they
were hopelessly and irretrievably beaten and
sent back to hell.

Captain Mahan has quoted the graphic account of the battle written by Lieutenant Paul
Harris Nicolas and published in 1829. The
young fellow's story (he was a lieutenant of marines, sixteen years old) runs thus: "As the
day dawned the horizon appeared covered with
ships. I was awakened by the cheers of the
crew, and by their rushing up the hatchways to
get a glimpse of the hostile fleet. The delight
manifested exceeded anything I ever witnessed,
surpassing even those gratulations when our
native cliffs are descried after a long period of
distant service. At nine we were about six
miles from them, with studding sails set on both

sides. The officers now met at breakfast, and
though each seemed to exult in the hope of a
glorious termination to the contest so near at
hand, a fearful presage was experienced that all
would not again unite at that festive board. One
was particularly impressed with a persuasion that
he should not survive the day. The sound of
the drum, however, soon put an end to our
meditations, and after a hasty, and alas ! a final
farewell to some, we repaired to our respective
posts. Our ship's station was far astern of our
leader, but her superior sailing caused an inter-
change of places with the 'Tonnant.' On our
passing that ship, the captains greeted each other
on the honourable prospect in view. Captain
Tyler ('Tonnant') exclaimed : 'A glorious day
for old England ! We shall have one a-piece
before to-night !' As if in confirmation of this
soul-inspiring sentiment the band of our consort was playing 'Britons strike home.'

"The drum now repeated its summons, and
the Captain sent for the officers commanding at
their several quarters. 'Gentlemen,' said he,
'I have only to say that I shall pass close under
the stern of that ship ; put in two round shot
and then a grape, and give her *that*. Now go
to your quarters, and mind not to fire until each
gun will bear with effect.' With this laconic

instruction the gallant little man posted himself on the side of the foremost carronade on the starboard side of the quarter-deck.

" From the peculiar formation of this part of the enemy's line as many as ten ships brought their broadside to bear with powerful effect. The determined and resolute countenance of the weather-beaten sailors, here and there brightened by a smile of exultation, was well suited to the terrific appearance which they exhibited. Some were stripped to the waist; some had bared their necks and arms; others had tied a handkerchief round their heads ; and all seemed eagerly to await the order to engage. The shot began to pass over us, and gave us an intimation of what we should in a few minutes undergo. An awful silence prevailed in the ship, only interrupted by the commanding voice of Captain Hargood, ' Steady! Starboard a little! steady so !' echoed by the master directing the quartermasters at the wheel. A shriek soon followed, a cry of agony was produced by the next shot, and the loss of a head of a poor recruit was the effect of the succeeding; and as we advanced destruction rapidly advanced.

" It was just twelve o'clock when we reached their line. Our energies became roused and the mind diverted from its appalling condition by the order of 'Stand to your guns!' which as they successively came to bear were discharged into our opponents on either side.   Although until that moment we had not fired a shot our sails and rigging bore evident proofs of the manner in which we had been treated; our mizzen-topmast was shot away and the ensign had thrice been re-hoisted.   The firing was now tremendous, and at intervals the dispersion of the smoke gave us a sight of the colours of our adversaries.

"At this critical period, whilst steering for the stern of the 'Indomptable,' which continued a most galling, raking fire upon us, the 'Fougueux' being on our starboard quarter and the Spanish 'San Justo' on our larboard bow, the master earnestly addressed the captain.   'Shall we go through, sir?'   'Go through by ———!' was his energetic reply.   'There's your ship, sir, place me close alongside of her.'   Our opponent defeated this manœuvre by bearing away in a parallel course with us within pistol-shot.

"About one o'clock the 'Fougueux' ran us on board the starboard side, and we continued thus engaging till the latter dropped astern. Our mizzenmast soon went, and soon afterwards the maintopmast.   A two-decked ship, the 'Neptune,' then took a position on our bow, and a seventy-four, 'Achille,' on our quarter.

At two o'clock the mainmast fell over our larboard side; I was at the time under the break of the poop, aiding in running out a carronade, when a cry of 'Stand clear there! here it comes!' made me look up, and at that instant the mainmast fell over the bulwarks just above me. This ponderous mass made the whole ship's frame shake, and had it taken a central direction it would have gone through the poop and added many to our list of sufferers. At half-past two our foremast was shot away close to the deck.

"In this unmanageable state we were but seldom capable of annoying our antagonists, while they had the power of choosing their distance, and every shot from them did considerable execution. Until half-past three we remained in this harassing situation. At this hour a three-decked ship was seen apparently steering towards us; it can easily be imagined with what anxiety every eye turned towards this formidable object, which would either relieve us from our unwelcome neighbours or render our situation desperate. We had scarcely seen the British colours since one o'clock, and it is impossible to express our emotion as the alteration of the stranger's course displayed the white ensign to our sight. Soon the 'Swiftsure' came nobly to our relief.

Can any enjoyment in life be compared with the sensation of delight and thankfulness which such a deliverance produced? On ordinary occasions we contemplate the grandeur of a ship under sail with admiration; but under impression of danger and excitement such as prevailed at this crisis every one eagerly looked toward our approaching friend, who came speedily on, and when within hail manned the rigging, cheered, and then boldly steered for the ship which had so long annoyed us.

"Before sunset all firing had ceased. The view of the fleet at this period was highly interesting, and would have formed a beautiful subject for a painter. Just under the setting rays were five or six dismantled prizes; on one hand lay the 'Victory' with part of our fleet and prizes, on the left hand the 'Sovereign' and a similar cluster of ships; the remnant of the combined fleet was making for Cadiz to the northward. The 'Achille' had burned to the water's edge with the tricoloured ensign still displayed, about a mile from us, and our tenders and boats were using every effort to save the brave fellows who had so gloriously defended her; but only two hundred and fifty were rescued, and she blew up with a tremendous explosion."

Nelson and Captain Hardy were walking the

deck of the "Victory" at about a quarter past one, while the battle all about still raged, when a ball struck him in the shoulder and penetrated his chest. He fell to the deck on his face. A sergeant of marines and two seamen raised him, stained with the blood of his own secretary, Scott, who had been killed on the spot a little while before. "They have done for me at last, Hardy," said Nelson. "I hope not," was the answer. "Yes," said he; "my backbone is shot through." They carried him down into the cock-pit, a gloomy abode indeed, hellish with the groans of the wounded, ghastly with the figures of the dying or the dead. One of the wounded called out to the surgeon, who had just examined two officers and found them lifeless: "Mr. Beatty, Lord Nelson is here. Mr. Beatty, the Admiral is wounded." He ran to Nelson's side. "Ah, Mr. Beatty," exclaimed the dying victor, "you can do nothing for me. I have but a short time to live." "Alas! Beatty, how prophetic you were!" cried Dr. Scott, referring to the apprehensions the surgeon had expressed for Nelson's safety, as he had throughout worn a coat conspicuous with orders upon it.

There is not a more affecting and tragic scene in the records of humanity than this great and glorious man's deathbed. Affecting it was, and no Englishman can read the description of it at this hour unmoved, because it was Nelson who lay dying; and it is tragic because of the red and thunderous frame it was set in. Dr. Scott, the chaplain, used to speak of the deck of the "Victory" as resembling a "butcher's shambles." He saw an officer in some frenzy of pain tear the ligatures from his wound and bleed to death. The ladder was slippery with blood. On deck all was uproar, shouts, the volcanic blast of guns, and smoke as thick as fog. Scott bent over the dying hero, who said in a low voice, "I leave Lady Hamilton and my adopted daughter, Horatia, as a legacy to my country." His constant cry was for drink, and they gave him lemonade and wine-and-water. The "Victory's" crew cheered whenever an enemy's ship struck. One of these huzzas reached Nelson's ears. Lieutenant Pasco, who lay wounded, answered his inquiry, and the news lighted up his pale face. He constantly asked for Captain Hardy, who at last arrived. They shook hands affectionately, and Nelson inquired how the battle went. Hardy answered that twelve or fourteen of the enemy's ships had struck. "I hope," said Nelson, "none of our ships have struck, Hardy?" "No, my Lord," replied Hardy, "there is no fear of that."

When Hardy made his second visit Nelson was still alive, and the Captain congratulated him, even in the moment of death, on his brilliant victory. He could not tell how many ships were taken; he believed fourteen or fifteen. "That is well," answered Nelson, "but I bargained for twenty;" and then emphatically exclaimed, "Anchor, Hardy, anchor." The dying hero could not then, perhaps, conceive that the ground tackle of most of the ships was in such a condition as to render anchoring impossible. Collingwood afterwards did not anchor, and has been blamed for the loss of many prizes. But he was a great sailor, and exactly knew what to do. And it is only writers ignorant of the difficulties and perils of the ocean, of shoals and lee shores, and heavy gales of wind, and crippled ships, some without steering gear, some sheer hulks, who would challenge the judgment of such a seaman as Collingwood, who was *there* and responsible!

"Doctor," said Nelson, turning to the Chaplain, "I have *not* been a *great* sinner." The Doctor rubbed the poor sufferer's body, and they often ejaculated short prayers together; and Nelson frequently said, "Pray for me, Doctor." The last words the Chaplain heard Nelson murmur were, "God and my country." And then

18

he peacefully died — so calmly that Scott, who was rubbing his breast, continued to chafe him for some minutes, unconscious that the end had come.

Thus died one of the most beautiful, noble, and heroic characters which this country has ever produced, or of which the history of the world makes any mention. No Englishman has left a more valuable memory. The name of Nelson is as magical to-day as it was when he was fighting the battles of his country. It is the inspiration of all that is honourable, fearless, patriotic, to the very crown and summit of the meaning of the words. He was as simple as a child, he was as tender and affectionate as a woman, and his heart was that of a lion. The material and moral debt of the country to this man is so great that when we seek for comparison in the services of even the most splendid and shining characters we find the appeal weak; the claim shrinks, even if it be a Wellington on whom our eyes are fixed, because in no one life will we discover combined all that Nelson did for England, and in no one human memory will we find the influence that he still exerts.

CHAPTER XII

POOR JACK

Preliminary Notice

In Nelson's time the Royal Navy was largely dependent upon the Merchant Service for the seamen who manned its ships. The wisdom of our forefathers provided for this by certain laws called the Navigation Acts. It was contrived that if a shipowner allowed one foreigner aboard his vessel he was forced by the Acts to take a certain number of Englishmen proportioned to the tonnage of the ship. This simple expedient kept up the supply of British sailors, and a finer race of Merchant Seamen than those which existed in Nelson's time never trod shipboard before or since. When the Navigation Laws were repealed, custom for some years clung, and the large full-rigged ships continued to put forth liberally manned. But by degrees the gangrene of managing ownership bit its way steadily into the vitals of the Merchant Service. The Managing Owner is a man without patriotism; he is concerned in dividends only. It is his business to make his "boat" "pay." Who will blame him? But the effect of competition has been to drive out the good English seamen and to let in the base foreigner. It cannot be long before the English seaman will to all intents and purposes cease to have existence. At the present time there are three hundred non-naturalised foreigners in *command* of ships in the British Mercantile Marine. How many mates and second mates I have not ascertained. The ship's forecastle is filled with the foreigner, but the shipowner, I believe, much as he admires the man's theories of cheap wage and unfit diet, has not thought proper yet to trust him with the engines. It seems to be a question of supreme importance, because I do not see where we are to turn unless to the Merchant Service for sailors to man our ships when men are wanted. It is useless to talk of the fishermen and the longshoremen. Nelson long ago discovered that there was no confidence to be reposed in that sort of people, and that though imminent and deadly as the peril apparently was, only the faintest response attended our hero's patriotic appeal to the men. The following article is reprinted from the " English Illustrated Magazine " (1896), and it fitly supplements a series of sketches of the career of a man whose victories were achieved by help of the merchant seamen who manned his fleets.

1897.

" Unless some provision is at once made for the training of boys the employment of foreign sailors must of necessity considerably increase ; and ten years hence, under present conditions, a British crew will be almost unobtainable. This matter requires to be dealt with immediately and on a large scale. *It is in the domestic affairs of the country the most vital question of the day.* . . . If the number of British seamen were sufficiently increased there would never be any difficulty in getting men for the Navy." — Mr. Joseph Hoult, " Manning Report," 1896.

I AM happy to find myself in accord with a gentleman who is so well known in shipping circles as Mr. Joseph Hoult of Liverpool. But how is it that Mr. Hoult has waited until now to make a discovery of imperial moment? Or, if before the current year he was sensible that the British merchant seaman was a decaying condition of our national life, why did not he put his alarms upon record? Why, as a patriot, which I am sure he is, should he persistently have kept the telescope at his blind eye! He doubtless understood, as did the rest of his fraternity, to what the encouragement of the foreigner to sail in British forecastles was tending.

In 1881 I left Newcastle-on-Tyne to settle in London. My professional obligations caused me to look very closely into the maritime life, and I then quite easily saw that if the British shipowner was not restricted in his employment of foreign labour the doom of our mercantile Jack was sealed. When the Shipping office was on Tower Hill, I visited that dismal haunt of the dejected, and often hopeless, English seaman: it was dirty and neglected; its grimy alcoves or shelters yawned in sullen sympathy with the weary mariner waiting for a ship. I spent some hours in that melancholy cavern, and stood a careful observer of what was passing. I took notice of a large number of foreigners, yellow-haired, freckled, self-confident, audacious in their knowledge that they were of the elect. I also observed that many of the English sea-

men, though poorly clad, and exhibiting other
marks of great poverty, were as likely a lot of
livelies as a sailor who knows the character of
sailors, who is fit to command sailors, could wish
to fill his forecastle with.   Yet what was my
experience?   Crew after crew of " Dutchmen "
were called in to " sign on."   Every time the
door was opened the English seamen darted
eager looks.   " Good God ! " I thought, " am
I in England ?   Is it imaginable that the ' bally
Scandyhoovian,' the Dago, the ' Dutchman,'
have gained a victory undreamt of by Tromp
and De Ruyter ! "   *Ex pede Herculem*.   I
seemed to find the magnificent industry which
had been built up by the British blood and by
the splendid seafaring qualities of the British
sailor in the hands of the foreigner, who was
good enough to allow us to continue to fly our
flag because our shipowners were considerate
enough to choose him, and feed him, and pay
him.

These kingdoms form the greatest maritime
nation that the world has ever beheld.   It is,
nevertheless, true that there is scarce a public in
Europe more ignorant of and indifferent to sea
affairs than the people of this country.   If you
speak to the man in the street about our Mercantile Marine he will look at you with a dull

and silly eye. Pronounce the word sailor, and
his imagination conjures up the bluejacket who
lurched against him round the corner yonder.
" Millions," wrote a shipowner to me, " have
never seen the ocean, much less ships. What,
then, should they know about the Mercantile
Marine?"   But there are millions who have
seen the ocean and travelled upon it; scores of
them keep yachts, scores have seats in the
House of Commons; and to these millions the
Mercantile Marine is as much an abstraction as
the Revenue was to Charles Lamb. The man
in the street, feeling unwell, resolves on a trip
to New York.   On his return he has seen
nothing but New York.   What has gone
between consists of certain dim sensations and
perceptions of nausea, meal-time, the smoking-
room, and large head seas.   Although he is
being swept onwards by a superb example of
our great national industry, he takes no count of
it. To him the captain is a man in buttons on
a bridge. Does the man in the street realise
the enormous responsibilities, moral and material, which that figure up there embodies — the
safety of the noble fabric, the precious lives of
perhaps a thousand people, cargo of the value
of a German principality ?   Does the man in the
street note the sailors who move about the decks

forward, the firemen, and others who rise, sweating and purple out of the hell in the deep bowels of the ship? He will tell you about Broadway, but he has not a syllable to utter on the subject of our Merchant Service and the sailors who navigated and worked the ship that conveyed him across the Atlantic and home.

Now, in making the above statement, I am quite convinced of its accuracy, and I am also persuaded that the ship-owning classes are likewise conscious that the man in the street heeds not, and knows nothing about, our Mercantile Marine. And so for years, taking advantage of an ignorance which is largely due to indifference, they have been insidiously sapping the life of the British merchant seaman by stealthy but insistent importation of the foreigner, whose recommendation, we are told, is that he is cheap, that he does not murmur when bad food is given to him, that he is tractable, and that ship-masters choose him in preference to their fellow-countrymen. To what issue? In " Brassey's Naval Annual " for 1895 it is stated, on an authority which the shipowners themselves do not resist, that our Mercantile Marine is manned by 235,000 men, of whom 55,000 *only* are British seamen! The statement proceeds: " This is but a little more than half of the Naval Reserve of France."

These were the figures in 1895. What will this year give us? And how will next year work out?[1] Of these 55,000 British sailors a large proportion are without work. This is clearly stated by a very intelligent writer in a shipping paper, Aug. 13, 1896: "How many thousand seamen are there at the present moment out of employment, and why don't they go to the Royal Navy if they have a turn that way? And if they have not a turn that way they are not likely to alter their minds, when by Mr. Clark Russell's plan there would be four-fold employment for them in the Mercantile Marine." I paused to explain that I never suggested a "fourfold employment." I had said that it was " our duty to foster the merchant seaman, to double him, to quadruple him." This could only be done by the elimination of the foreign element from our forecastles. Ships might go undermanned as they are, but still, by getting rid of your foreigners you would speedily treble and quadruple your British merchant seaman. It stands to reason that the thousands of English sailors who cannot obtain employment because of the forecastle being filled with foreign

[1] This year (1897) the number is 30,000.

labour must either starve and die or seek work ashore; or if they continue sailors they will not serve under the commercial flag of this country. The process of diminution then is steady, and unless the decay is arrested promptly, and by imperial measures, the country will find itself face to face with a condition that to my mind is little less than appalling — I mean the total and, I fear, the irremediable extinction of the British merchant seaman.

Is the country willing that he should be extinguished? Are we content to reflect that the day is not far distant when our steamers and sailing-ships will be entirely manned by foreigners? Mr. Goschen, one of the shrewdest of politicians, seems of opinion that the Mercantile Marine cannot any longer be considered as a source for drafts for the Royal Navy. I hold, therefore, that the shipowners who are desperately jealous of the encroachment of the foreigner upon their trade will be responsible, themselves only, for the annihilation of what I have always regarded as our second line of defence.

Our forefathers manifestly understood the traditional character of the shipowner better than we do: they provided against the failure of those patriotic sentiments which should animate

us all by certain enactments which figure in
history as the Navigation Laws. Under those
laws a shipowner, if he entered but one foreign
sailor, was compelled to ship one British seaman
to every twenty tons; and in no case was the
foreign element allowed to exceed one fourth of
the whole. Thus a ship of one thousand tons
would sail with fifty British seamen in her forecastle, and her owner would probably not think
any addition necessary to that complement in
the shape of the foreigner. The wisdom of this
provision was again and again illustrated. Lord
Howe's great and important victory of June 1
was gained chiefly by the merchant seamen of
the kingdom. When the war broke out in 1793
we had not forty-five thousand men, and they
were scattered over the globe. The merchant
service enabled us swiftly to man some sixty sail
of the line and double the number of frigates
and smaller vessels. Some thirty-five thousand
or forty-five thousand seamen of the Mercantile
Marine were rapidly brought together; and
these men, in addition to those in the Service,
enabled Admiral Gardner to proceed to the
West Indies with seven sail of the line; and
Lord Hood, with twenty-two sail of the line, to
the Mediterranean, to occupy Toulon and capture Corsica. Other squadrons were sent to

America and the East Indies to protect our
interests in those quarters; and Lord Howe
guarded the Channel with twenty-seven sail of
the line.

I shall be told that the manning of the war-
ships was due to the pressgangs.   But the
sources of supply were there!   Collingwood's
ship, the " Royal Sovereign," that was ahead of
the other British vessels at Trafalgar by a quarter of an hour or twenty minutes, was filled with
merchant men from the Tyne Side, and how
those seamen spoke in their guns whilst the
noble old Admiral paced the deck munching an
apple, all who have read the thrilling story of
the most glorious of sea-fights will know.

Steam, of course, has greatly modified the
duties of the sea career.   But there still remains
a small tonnage in sail from which the foreigner
should be rigorously excluded.   And the steam-
boat will always be in need of sailors; there is,
indeed, nothing to do aloft; but the lead, the
look-out, the boats, the helm, tending the small
canvas the vessel may carry, are sailors' work,
and no other labourer springing on board off
the edge of a wharf would be fit for it.   There
are many duties on board a steamer which seamen alone can discharge.   Mr. G. A. Laws, General Manager of the Shipping Federation, and

one of the ablest of the exponents of the interests
of the shipowners, seems of opinion that seamen
will not be required for the Navy. I recall this
singular statement because I regard it as expressing, but not explaining, the motive of the
shipowners' neglect of the merchant seaman.
Mr. Laws says that the captain of an ironclad
will carry her into action with marine gunners,
marines, engineers, and stokers. *C'est tout!* no
bluejackets! Who is to man the boats? Who
is to take possession? What body of men
are to be thrown ashore to fight side by side
with the marines? Who, in short, of Mr.
Laws' crew are to take the place of our naval
seamen?

If the shipowners are permitted to extinguish
the sailor they will repel the rising youth of this
country, and English boys will not go to sea
because their fathers would easily perceive that
they had more reasonably dedicated them to the
life of the crossing and the broom than to a
profession from which they will be swiftly expelled by the foreigner. The shipowners com-
plain of over-legislation, but it seems to me that
they are ceaselessly provoking it. Even as I
write legislation may be in the air in respect of
a new manning scale. And should this happen,
further legislation may be threatening, for it

cannot be doubted that the public, when it is
tardily made to understand that the seaman is a
decaying factor, and must presently be as dead
as the dodo, will insist upon the Legislature
going to work to resuscitate and enlarge him
into all necessary plenty.   It may be done!
Our forefathers did it.   A few years of fostering
would fill London and the outports with British
seamen.   The forecastle would cease to be a
menagerie.   The red flag would float in pride,
and the country would have its own again.

As the seaman is an uneducated man in the
main — there are many exceptions — he cannot
make his grievances understood nor his wishes
felt, either in print or by speech.   He forms
into processions, but these tedious trudgings are
bitterly aimless for want of profitable govern-
ance.   I have been much scorned and derided
by the shipping Press for speaking of Jack's
" characteristic simplicity " and " childlike nature," but am I the inventor or the discoverer
of these qualities in the seaman ?   Is it not these
very traits of character which have endeared
him to his countrymen, and rendered him the
most popular of all the toilers on this toilsome
globe ?   From the days of the coracle the seaman's trusting, generous, open nature has been
the burden of the ballad and the song, and you

will find it described at large in works written and published long before I was in petticoats. It is the confiding and simple character of the seaman which the owner has taken advantage of. He fed him as he pleased till the law stepped in. He sent him to sea in rotting hulls, and again the law stepped in. He sends him to sea in sailing ships whose crews are all too few, and in steamers to be, by his paucity, a source of terror on the ocean highway.

When the Sailors' and Firemen's Association was established my best wishes attended it, though knowing that the sailor's life was inevitably errant and fugitive, I feared that combination would be impracticable. How can a man combine who cannot live unless he goes away? Still, I trusted that the representatives he left behind would serviceably, patiently, and always honourably seek to promote his interests. It is many years now since I received this letter: —

NORTH OF ENGLAND SAILORS' AND FIREMEN'S ASSOC.,
130, High Street, Sunderland, Dec. 5, 1884.

Dear Sir, — I have been authorised by the above Society to ask you if you would be so kind as to represent our Society along with Mr. T. Burt on the Commission for Shipping. We nominate you. Please let us know as soon as possible. — I am, yours truly,

S. J. PETTY, *Secretary*.

My professional duties obliged me to decline, but in the desire to contribute something towards a movement which I considered good and hopeful, I wrote an article in the " Contemporary Review," which I called " A Forecastle View of the Shipping Commission." This article brought me a letter from the late Mr. Thomas Gray, of the Board of Trade, asking me for a private interview. I was unable to comply, but I regret now that I did not make the acquaintance of a gentleman whose sympathies very strongly inclined towards seamen. For some years I followed the proceedings of the Union with interest ; but when it came to the unmanly and brutal system of the picket and to exactions on the pocket of the seaman, I own that I was repelled ; I could find nothing in this form of unionism to commend itself to any theory of action calculated to prove of real and lasting benefit to the merchant sailor. A policy of rabid aggression could end in nothing but the alienation of public sympathy. It was hard that seamen, thousands of miles distant, should be held responsible for the actions of those who were said to represent them ashore. As in law a man is bound by his agent, so by society is he taken at the value of the representation he submits. I do not suppose that the labours of

unionism where docks and seamen are concerned
can be pursued with hands in kid gloves; but
prudence surely should have dictated limitations,
seeing that the contest is between great poverty
and great wealth; and the policy that forced the
shipowners to combine for the preservation of
their imperilled property was ill-judged.

The Shipping Federation is the combination
I refer to. It is an association of owners and
managers, who, in spite of the spirit of competition which makes them love one another much
as Mrs. Gamp loved humanity (" I could lay
'em all out for nothing, sich is the love I bears
'em "), formed into a phalanx, and in grim array,
bristling with weapons of shipping offices, Federation tickets, and the like, hissed defiance at
the Union and bade it come on. It did come
on, but only to break itself into pieces as the
roller plunging at the base of the rock recoils in
shattered waters.

We are being constantly reminded that the
shipping industry is in a semi-insolvent state,
and those who make us acquainted with this
dark and dreary condition of things send their
letters to the newspapers from great West-End
squares, and from mansions in London and
from manors in the provinces. No one need
doubt that just at present a certain class of

owner is not saving very much money—he is
not, in short, growing rapidly wealthy.   To
him belongs the steam-tramp, the cheaply built
and heavily burdened boat, whose launch added
a new terror to the many which old ocean
has created for the discomfiture of man.   The
owner of one boat— I might easily say two, but
will call it one — is typically a gentleman whose
sense of moral obligations is created by the
Shipping Acts.   If there were no Acts he would
have no sense of moral obligations.   Very lean
does he keep the duties imposed upon him by
law.   He would starve them if he durst.   With
him and in his boat the hungry British ship-
master, so that he may obtain employment,
invests his poor savings — money gained by
years of such labour and anxieties as there is no
virtue in the pen to communicate.   He is defrauded ; others who have invested are defrauded.
But before this has happened, possibly the
cargo-tank, made wicked by frequent visits of
the managing owner, has sunk two or three good
ships, and imperilled the safety of a liner with
two hundred and eighty thousand pounds in
specie aboard.   Why not?   The gentleman
whose moral obligations are entirely statutory
has sent her to sea so undermanned that she is a
menace to everything that crosses her bows.

Four sailors in the forecastle — two in a watch! an officer, who dare not tell the truth for fear of being dismissed, on the bridge, and this gallant ship may be fifteen hundred tons, and her official number can be read in " Mitchell's List."

I am asked how I connect the ocean tramp with that decay of the British merchant sailor which I am lamenting. I answer by saying that if you step on board one of these vessels you will be saluted by the German mate in broken English, and that if you go forward the first man you speak to will scarcely understand you because he is a Russian Finn, and the second man you address is a Dane, and a third some strange, wild mixture of black and white blood, of a nation indeterminable, but of considerable capacities where his sheath-knife fits the hip. Three to one, — for the fourth shall be an Englishman, — in this noble ship's company; for it is true that even from the meanest forecastle under the British flag the foreigner is expelling the Englishman.

Was it for the Dutchman and for the splendid services he rendered this country that Campbell wrote that noble lyric " Ye Mariners of England"? Was it for the Dago and the Finn that the same fine poet composed those thrilling verses beginning, —

Men of England ! who inherit
Rights that cost your sires their blood ?

I cannot but write with some heat when I think
of this foreign invasion, and reflect upon the
Germans' and the "Scandyhoovians'" appro-
priation of Jack's heritage. The shipowners
must not whine an apology for an extinction
whose effect they will be the first to feel, and
which many are now viewing with ill-dissembled
alarm, by pleading that our sailors are not the
men our forefathers were. This assurance may
be dismissed with contempt. The seaman of
to-day is as able, high-spirited, and alert a man
as ever sailed to the Indies last century, as ever
helped thrash the Spaniard up-Channel round
into the North Sea. But what chance do you
give him? You put him into an undermanned
ship; a heavily large proportion of his shipmates
are of different nationalities. One swallow does
not make a summer. One or two able British
seamen will not make a good crew. In short,
the shipowners do not require the services of
the English sailor, and I am very sorry to say
that their destructive neglect of the man is backed
by the submissive acquiescence of the British
shipmaster. No doubt much of the support
the shipowners are receiving in their efforts to
surpress our native seamen is due to the ship-

master's fear of being dismissed; therefore, in order to earn his bread he continues to choose foreign crews, smacks his lips over them, professes to relish them; but if he has crawled through the hawse-pipe, as he doubtless has, he lies in his heart, and knows that he lies, when he affirms that a crew of mixed nationalities is superior to a crew of English sailors. That the ship-master is constrained by fear and will not speak the truth because his berth is his life I am convinced by this token: that, when he quits the sea and settles down with a telescope in some little 'longshore home called "The Perch" or "The Cabin," he will not suffer a syllable to be said against the British seaman. Independence matures the spirit of loyalty, and he is faithful then in his sentiments to his flag and his country.

I have dealt with a question that is not generally understood, and it is not in the power of a single pen to make itself felt and heard over the wide area of interests which the subject concerns. The great public Press of this country, the directors and the expositors of public opinion, should deal with the decay of the British merchant seaman as with something of supreme national moment, annually growing in urgency. I repeat what I have elsewhere said: the foreigner must be as severely restricted by legisla-

tion as he was by the Navigation Acts, and
every encouragement should be given to our
merchant sailors to multiply, that we may point
to them with the same spirit of patriotic pride
with which we survey the league-long line of
mighty ironclads, but mighty only in the men
that man them.

SUPPLEMENTARY NOTE

IF no hero was ever more mourned it must be said that no hero was ever more honoured in his death. The news of the victory electrified the country, but the deep sensations of triumph were subdued by the chilling grief of an irreparable loss. The Park and Tower guns thundered the news to the Londoners. On hearing of the death of Lord Nelson the King seemed so deeply affected that a silence of nearly five minutes ensued. The Queen called the Princesses round her and read the despatches aloud and the Royal group wept.

This story is told of Mr. Pitt, the Prime Minister, by Lord Malmesbury: "On the receipt of the news of the memorable battle of Trafalgar (some day in November, 1805), I happened to dine with Pitt and it was naturally the engrossing subject of our conversation. I shall never forget the eloquent manner in which he described his conflicting feelings when roused in the night to read Collingwood's despatches. Pitt observed that he had been called up at various hours in his eventful life by the arrival of news of various hues, but that whether good or bad he could always lay his head on his pillow and sink into sound sleep again. On this occasion, however, the great event announced brought with it so much to weep over, as well as to rejoice at, that he could not calm his thoughts, but at length got up, though it was three in the morning."

The "Victory" arrived, with the body of Nelson on board, at Spithead on the 5th December. The corpse had been enclosed in a cask,* from which it was removed to a plain elm coffin under a canopy of colours. Every Admiral in the British Navy received an invitation to attend Nelson's funeral. The Chief Mourner was Nelson's early friend, Sir Peter Parker, the venerable Admiral of the Fleet. It is stated in the Annual Register: "When the Duke of Clarence ascended the steps of St. Paul's, he suddenly stopped, and took hold of the colours that were borne by the 'Victory's' men, and after conversing with one of the gallant tars, he burst into tears. On the entrance of the tattered flags within the communion rail the Prince of Wales, after conversing with the Duke of Clarence, sent and requested that they might be brought as near the grave as possible, and on

* THE BODY OF NELSON HAD BEEN KEPT IN A RUM BARREL FOR THE LONG VOYAGE HOME.

observing them, although at some distance, the tears fell from his Royal Highness."

It is pleasant to think that though the Rev. William Nelson was presented with an Earldom, Lady Nelson was not forgotten. On the 1st February she was thus distinguished by a message from the Crown: "His Majesty having taken into His Royal consideration the splendid and unparalleled achievements of the late Vice-Admiral Lord Viscount Nelson, Knight of the Most Hon. Order of the Bath, during a life spent in the service of his country, and terminated in the moment of victory by a glorious death, and being desirous of conferring on his relict Lady Viscountess Nelson a nett annuity of £2,000 per annum for the term of her natural life, recommends it to his faithful Commons to consider of a proper method of enabling His Majesty to grant such annuity, and of securing and settling the same in such manner as shall be thought most effectual for the benefit of the said Lady Viscountess Nelson. G.R."

It was felt by Lord Collingwood as a hardship that his title was restricted to his life. He was practically divorced from his wife for years, owing to his being ceaselessly engaged in blockading; and he had but two daughters, through whom the title did not descend.

A curious account of Lady Hamilton is related in the life of the Reverend Dr. Scott.   It
runs thus: "It may be supposed that, after
Scott's return from sea, he had little wish, as he
had little opportunity, for renewing his association with Lady Hamilton.   He had known her
well during his intimacy with his lamented pa-
tron (Nelson), and had been the frequent witness
of her peculiar fascinations.   She had an heroic
spirit, great personal attractions and much clev-
erness, and at Merton, in Clarges Street, and
in Piccadilly, where Scott was frequently sum-
moned to participate in the festivities, or to assist on important occasions of business, he had
admired her many accomplishments, and been
amused by her dramatic personating of different
characters.   Though the country did nothing
for her, she was left at Lord Nelson's death with
means sufficient to fulfil his wishes in the education of Horatia, having at least £1,400 a year,
besides the little estate at Merton, but her vanity and extravagance found this no competency.
A friend of the Merton coterie was one day
hailed from a carriage window in London by
the voice of a lady, whom he recognised as
Lady Hamilton, and who immediately requested
him to return home with her to dinner.   He
pleaded an engagement, but was obliged to

promise to visit Merton the following day. He
had no expectation of meeting any company,
and was therefore not a little astonished on
his arrival to find what guests were assembled.
Signor Rovedino and Madame Bianchi, with
other birds of the same feather, were regaled
by her ladyship, on this occasion, with a sumptu-
ous dinner: and, after the ladies retired, the superb wines of the Merton cellars, gifts of crowned
heads, etc., were liberally dispensed by Rovedino, as master of the ceremonies. The friend
we have alluded to was in the garden next morning, long before the breakfast hour, and was at
length joined there by Lady Hamilton, with
whom he ventured to remonstrate on the mode
of life she was pursuing, and the company she
had treated him with. She attempted to justify
herself by saying that 'it was a less expensive
plan than taking Horatia to town for singing
and Italian lessons.' Her friend, however,
would not admit her excuse, and at length ex-
torted the sorrowful confession that her affairs
were already in a state of grievous embarrass-
ment. He talked seriously and sincerely with
her, and agreed to find the means of relieving
her. In a few days they had another interview,
when he introduced a gentleman who had retired from commercial engagements, but was

well skilled in all matters of finance, and who undertook, on Lady Hamilton's promising to comply with his conditions, to investigate the whole state of her affairs, and remedy them, if it were possible. On looking into them he found that two or three years' retirement in Wales upon a small annuity would suffice to release her from all difficulties. Into Wales she accordingly went, but it was only for a short season; the harp and the viol were soon resounding from her lighted apartments in Bond Street, wilder extravagances than ever were committed, and she was again a suppliant for relief to the friends whose advice she had disregarded. The financier was again appealed to; but this time he refused his aid, avowing openly that all attempts to save a person of her character must be in vain. Distress soon after pursued her abroad: and it is well known that she died in great poverty, having gone through one of the most extraordinary careers that ever fell to the lot of her sex."

Lady Hamilton was buried just outside Calais. When the news of her death reached England a Mr. H. Cadogan and Earl Nelson went over to Calais, "where," says Mr. W. H. Long, "the former paid the funeral expenses of the deceased, which amounted to £28.10, and

on his return brought her daughter Horatia back
to her native land with him." This young lady
married the Reverend Philip Ward, sometime
vicar of Tenterten in Kent. She died, aged
eighty-one, March 6, 1881.

The Naval Institute Press is the book-publishing arm of the U.S. Naval Institute, a private, nonprofit, membership society for sea service professionals and others who share an interest in naval and maritime affairs. Established in 1873 at the U.S. Naval Academy in Annapolis, Maryland, where its offices remain today, the Naval Institute has members worldwide.

Members of the Naval Institute support the education programs of the society and receive the influential monthly magazine *Proceedings* and discounts on fine nautical prints and on ship and aircraft photos. They also have access to the transcripts of the Institute's Oral History Program and get discounted admission to any of the Institute-sponsored seminars offered around the country.

The Naval Institute also publishes *Naval History* magazine. This colorful bimonthly is filled with entertaining and thought-provoking articles, first-person reminiscences, and dramatic art and photography. Members receive a discount on *Naval History* subscriptions.

The Naval Institute's book-publishing program, begun in 1898 with basic guides to naval practices, has broadened its scope to include books of more general interest. Now the Naval Institute Press publishes about one hundred titles each year, ranging from how-to books on boating and navigation to battle histories, biographies, ship and aircraft guides, and novels. Institute members receive significant discounts on the Press's more than eight hundred books in print.

Full-time students are eligible for special half-price membership rates. Life memberships are also available.

For a free catalog describing Naval Institute Press books currently available, and for further information about subscribing to *Naval History* magazine or about joining the U.S. Naval Institute, please write to:

Customer Service
U.S. Naval Institute
291 Wood Road
Annapolis, MD 21402-5034
Telephone: (800) 233-8764
Fax: (410) 269-7940
Web address: www.navalinstitute.org